notes from hell

a bulgarian nurse in libya

Valya Chervenyashka

with

Nikolay Yordanov

30° South Publishers

Published in 2010 by 30° South Publishers (Pty) Ltd.
3 Ajax Place, 120 Caroline Street, Brixton
Johannesburg 2092, South Africa
www.30degreessouth.co.za
info@30degreessouth.co.za

Design and origination by 30° South Publishers (Pty) Ltd.

Cover image © Ingram Publishing

Printed and bound by Pinetown Printers, Durban

978-1920143-47-3

To my husband Emil, for nothing stopped him until he got me back into his life. To all those who thought about us, who sent us cards, letters and gifts, while we were condemned as murderers. To all those who were diagnosed with HIV and to those who still live with it. To all people in this world who are unjustly sentenced or imprisoned and suffer unjustly.

Contents

Introduction

… Then he slapped me. He barked something in Arabic and they all immediately surrounded me. They dragged me to the corridor again. The ropes tightened around my wrists. They tied them around my ankles too and hung me upside down.

"Well, now you're going to tell us everything!" my tormentor growled. He pulled out a thick cable wrapped in black insulation and whipped me. The first blow cut through my heels with a pain I had never experienced. This was just the beginning of what was to become the longest night of my life.

Hello! My name is Valya Chervenyashka. Maybe you have heard about me. I was born in the small, poor town of Vratsa in Bulgaria. I am a nurse by profession. I am fifty-four years old. I spent eight years behind the bars of several Libyan prisons, accused of mass murder. I have been sentenced to death three times. Coarse voices have cursed me, unknown people's hands have assaulted my body, hundreds of throats have yelled my name, thousands of hearts have passionately bayed for my death and millions of people from countries all over the world have seen my face …

I often think about the past. I am a woman who has come back from hell. I am tormented by the fact that I was sent to prison only on account of fate and due to the criminal negligence of people I do not know. Despite everything you may have read about me in newspapers or seen on television, I wasn't the villain; I was the victim.

Maybe you have heard my story. Maybe you have read the facts. Let me tell you; you have no idea what it is like to walk in my shoes. I will tell you everything. This is the story of the most dreadful eight years of my life. I never thought I would experience something worth telling in a book. Honestly, I would prefer that nobody knew about me. I would prefer an ordinary life of small hardships and small joys. My experiences have transformed me into a macabre sort of celebrity. Today there are few doors closed to me. I know many people in many powerful places and few are indifferent to me and my story.

If only I could forget … but I can't. So I feel compelled to tell my story. I cannot forget these memories and I cannot walk away from them. I know that only by setting them free, will I free myself.

Arrival in Libya

I first saw Libya on 4 December 1984. I lived in communist Bulgaria and any escape—even to a totalitarian country such as Libya—was seen as a great opportunity. I left first and several months later Emil, my husband, came to join me. I went there to expand my horizons and to gain work experience.

I became a nurse by chance. I had applied for a course at the Sports Institute but neither my friend nor I were accepted. She suggested that we enrol somewhere else, study with gusto and then reapply the following year. That's how I came to study nursing.

Indeed, the next year she started studying at the Sports Institute but I continued to study to become a nurse. I liked it and I grew to love my profession. I became a paediatric nurse because I first started work in a paediatric department and I relished the feeling that I was helping children. I love kids.

In Bulgaria you don't earn much as a nurse so when the opportunity to go to Libya and earn good money was presented to me, I took it.

On my first visit to Libya I went to Tarhuna. I started working in a 'Bulgarian' hospital, so named because all my colleagues were Bulgarian and everything at the hospital was to our standards. It was a new, modern hospital. It was really clean and sterile. There were of course some local doctors as well, but they adopted our style of work: sheets were changed regularly, only disposable needles were used and parents could only visit their children twice a week. I was very happy there. The job was interesting, the conditions were perfect and the pay was good. Their country seemed ordered and things ran smoothly.

I was used to doing without, so the fact that the shops held little more than rice, tomato purée, sugar and salt, was of little concern to me. I had come from a country where you had to save for years to buy a car and obtaining a permanent telephone number was virtually impossible. Of course things are very different now; now you can buy anything, anywhere. The Libyan people and their way of life were very different. I accepted that, but I could never have suspected that these were the differences that would cost me dearly in the years to come.

While there, I endeavoured to learn a bit of Arabic so that I could communicate with the local doctors and the patients. For the most part I learned from the children in the wards. I used to ask them questions— one about his name; another whether she was okay; what did they call this or that—so that little by little I started to understand and speak a few words.

I kept only good memories from my stay there and when our contracts ended some two and a half years later, Emil and I left Libya on 5 May 1987. I thought it would be forever.

After the fall of communism life was hard in Bulgaria. My husband insisted that we go abroad again, because the money we earned in Bulgaria was nowhere near enough for us to make ends meet. I wasn't very keen, but Emil was insistent. A former Bulgarian colleague of mine, Vilma, was working in Libya at the time and she warned me that things had deteriorated and that the salaries had decreased significantly. We were not to be discouraged though—we would still earn more there than in Bulgaria.

It was in 1991 that Emil first suggested we go to Libya again, but somehow there was always something that prevented us from leaving. I got a visa in the early 1990s and just before we were to leave, my daughter Tony had a car accident. Naturally we stayed. By 1996, everything had been arranged by the state company that had coordinated our first trip to Libya. Then my mother died—unexpectedly. A doctor, a friend of ours, said, "It seems you're not destined to go there. This is God's way of telling you that you don't belong there. These are omens—first your child, now your mom."

I took no heed of those sage words. We were determined to make the trip so that we could finance our children's tertiary studies. At the beginning of 1998 both of my daughters had enrolled in the local university. There was no way we could afford their tuition on our salaries. So, with a view to securing funds to pay for university fees, I finally left for Libya, with the plan being that Emil would follow shortly after.

I arrived in Libya on 3 February 1998. I was allocated to Benghazi but I didn't want to go there because it was not possible for a second member of the family to work in the same city and I didn't want to be there without my husband. Finally, he convinced me that he would bribe someone and would join me later—that's the way things worked in Bulgaria in those days. Many people told me: "It's not a nice city. Don't go there. Conditions are not good ..." However, I was convinced that they were being overly cautious. After all, I had already travelled and worked in Libya and hadn't experienced any problems.

I went with a group of sixty-five people, comprising five doctors and sixty nurses. For twenty days we stayed in a nurses' hostel while awaiting reallocation. While there, I befriended some like-minded colleagues who had also come to Libya because they could earn more money than in Bulgaria.

One of my colleagues was called Rumyana. We had travelled to Libya together and we shared a room at the hostel, along with three other women. Over lunch at the hostel canteen one day, we struck up a conversation that was to lay the foundation for a firm friendship.

Rumyana had a unique talent and regularly performed 'coffee readings'. Just as palm readers 'divine' one's destiny using the lines of one's hands, Rumyana could 'predict' the future based on the dregs of one's coffee. I am not a superstitious person, so I really didn't give much thought to her dire prophesy: "You'll have problems in one year's time, major problems with the police." She was very insistent and every time we drank coffee together she reiterated her vision of doom for me. I thought there must be something psychologically wrong with her and told her so. I always speak my mind and I am not afraid of conflict. I must say what I think and then leave it to the future to reveal whether I am right or wrong. Good naturedly, she didn't take offence.

She relentlessly looked at the bottom of my coffee mug in an effort to 'see' a different outcome. I thought that she must have got it wrong. What nonsense she spoke ... Despite this aversion to her coffee readings, we remained friends even when we were allocated to different hospitals. Rumyana was sent to the surgery and I ended up in the children's department of the El-Fatih Hospital.

I first entered the El-Fatih Children's Hospital in Benghazi seventeen days after my arrival. I immediately realized that Libyan health care had changed a lot—and not for the better. I was appalled to see how filthy it was. There were no disposable sheets and no basic necessities for work. All the children had a few bedraggled companions in tow, which increased the risk of contamination and infection; they were also using rags from their homes as bedspreads and everything was tainted by a smell reminiscent of some kind of oil. The hygiene of the patients was disheartening too—some were clean, while others exuded the pungent smell of sickness. This hospital's vision of cleanliness differed vastly from mine and, overall, the hospital environment didn't meet European standards. Benghazi is one of the largest Libyan cities and was a former capital. At that time though, the country was under embargo, which, they told us, was why the dismal conditions existed, why there were no supplies and little or no medicines.

Our routine was simple: a day shift, night shift, then two days off. I was in a team with one Filipino girl and two girls from Libya. Sometimes we made appointments and at other times we administered medicine, admitted children or measured temperatures. The very manner in which the work was organized, with each team member taking turns to perform the various tasks, should have rendered the charges later brought against me baseless.

The worst workers were the Filipino ladies. They did as they pleased and they were dirty. Their poor hygiene habits carried over to their behaviour at the hospital. They didn't comply with the sterility requirements and often re-used the disposable supplies. It was inconceivable to the Bulgarian nurses that they re-use syringes. In Bulgaria, sterilizing instruments before using them was a rule you never violated. In Libya, however, the nurses decided how they would conduct themselves, often to the detriment of the patient. Many times we told the Filipino and Libyan ladies that re-using syringes was a dangerous practice, but they retorted, "You do as you know; we are responsible for ourselves!" No matter how many times we told them off, they wouldn't admit they were doing anything wrong.

After three months, although everybody was saying Emil would not get a visa for Libya, he came to join me. My friend Rumyana read his cup of coffee for clues to our future—with the same results—big problems with the authorities or the police in one year's time. Her prediction gnawed at me and I wondered what these 'problems' with the police could possibly be. I pondered the timeframe too. Why would whatever trouble that was heading our way only surface after a year? If there was something wrong with our visas, it would emerge much earlier, I thought. Gradually I stopped paying attention to this prophesied misfortune. I had too much work at the hospital to occupy my mind with something that seemed so ridiculous.

The hospital would give you self-catering accommodation which was little more than a room, but your husband couldn't stay with you. Emil had nowhere to live and during the first month together we chose to live illegally with a colleague of mine; Galya from Vratsa. We knew each other because we were from the same town. Although she already had several roommates, she still agreed to give us shelter. I vaguely knew one of the other housemates, Nasya Nenova, although we would only later get to know each other well.

It was really crowded because there were eight of us and there was a shortage of beds. We would have to take turns to sleep in the beds, which we did when others were away working night shifts. The hospital authorities had it within their power to provide us with accommodation but my requests were always met with the consistent refrain that there were no rooms available. We longed for a place of our own and after several weeks Emil and I found a house to rent. Although it was much more expensive than living at Galya's 'commune', renting a house meant that we could finally lead a relatively ordinary life.

On the days when I wasn't working in the hospital I cleaned the house of a Libyan family with eight children. The mother's name was Fatma. They lived near our house, in the next street. Our houses were back to back.

Not only did I clean their home, I was also like a mother to the children. When they were left at home, alone—sometimes for days at a time because their parents travelled a lot—I looked after them. Most of the children were already teenagers and only two were still very young. My job was to do the laundry every other day and to clean the rooms. As their house was huge and needed a lot of maintenance, Emil used to help.

There was an easy camaraderie and I regarded them as friends. I was even invited to sleep at their house a few times.

The family had no problem with the fact that we were Christian and accepted that our ways were different from their own. For instance, they never asked me to put on a headscarf, as is customary.

That was my everyday life. How could I have known that for months I had been followed by invisible eyes at the hospital? That secret plans were being laid; that there were lives fading away and someone had to pay for them; that soon my existence would be shaken and irrevocably changed. Although only an ordinary nurse, I would be transformed into a woman that some cursed and for whom others wept.

Infection

My favourite child in the ward was Ahmed. He was four or five years old and was very cute. I think that he initially made such a strong impression on me because he was such a happy and cheerful boy. I remember clearly the first time I saw him. I was walking along the corridor when I noticed a little boy following me. I asked him what his name was and before long Ahmed shadowed me whenever I conducted my rounds.

I paid more attention to him because he usually didn't have friends to visit, which was the norm with the older children. He had been placed with the children with disabilities and I felt sorry for him because he was obviously lonely. I often went to check how he was doing and to have a friendly word. All the other nurses liked him too and hung his picture up in the ward. He had a lung disease and it later turned out that he was HIV-positive.

During his stay at the hospital I became well acquainted with his mother, who was Egyptian. She was very grateful to me for taking a special interest in her son's welfare. She repeatedly told me that he regarded me as his best friend. I had no idea that she would one day give false testimony against me and be instrumental in sending me to prison.

Ashur was another of my favourites. He was a baby—only a few months old. He was soft-featured and plump. He was not popular with the nurses like Ahmed was and none of them wanted to connect his IV because they struggled to find his veins. Only I managed to do it without problems and his mother always begged me: "Please, sister, go to him; you know how to do it." I met his father as well. I saw Ashur often and became very attached to him. After a while it turned out that he was also HIV-positive.

There were also those children who practically lived in the ward, like Jamelia and Walid. They suffered from a rare dermatological disease called 'fish skin'. It is genetically inherited and inflicts terrible damage upon the body. I took the boys' fate to heart because few people at the hospital wanted to work with them, especially with Walid, who had been abandoned by his parents. I had a big soft spot for this teenager and paid him special attention as he was completely helpless. I even changed his soiled diapers and fed him as he could not do so himself. He could not walk and was confined to a wheelchair. Although it was difficult for him to talk, he managed somehow. So I taught him to speak a little Bulgarian and told him stories about my home country. The Polish ladies had also taught him a few Polish words and he learned some English too.

The nurses were afraid of Walid and some were repulsed by his condition. Some behaved as though he was a monster. He presented a terrible picture—he had no hair and smelt like a swamp because of the fish oil we regularly rubbed him with. It didn't matter to me that he was ugly and that he looked scary; I could tell that he was a very smart and alert kid. I loved him and I often hugged him. Starved for affection, he always asked me: "Can I touch you, can I kiss you ..." and I always let him, to the dismay of some of my colleagues.

He desperately needed to be loved, as most people shied away from him. When I embraced him, he would protest: "But you will be all covered in oil!"

"It doesn't matter. I will wash myself later!" I would reply.

I was his only friend and he craved my company. When I was busy in other wards, he often looked for me, going from room to room in his wheelchair. The poor thing even used the elevator to get to other floors to see me.

I cared for many children in the hospital and their faces and stories still crowd my memories. Some of these children's fates are interwoven with my own and we share a devastating drama.

◈ ◈ ◈

The HIV virus spread through the El-Fatih Hospital at an alarming rate. The first time we became aware that there was a problem was when a child called Soad tested positive for HIV when having a compulsory AIDS test before an operation. The doctors reported the case to the children's hospital. The ward boss subsequently insisted that all the staff be tested for HIV.

We were all tested and all our results were negative. They also tested the staff in some of the other wards and all those results were negative as well. A head nurse called Amina came to us and ordered us to test all children in the ward. When we asked to see the results, she refused. However, from time to time we did come across the children's test results in the course of our work, but they were always negative. Looking back, it is obvious that the positive ones were kept well away from us. We didn't know at that stage that we had an epidemic on our hands, but perhaps we should have. Amina would often tell us that, "Another child tested positive. Work with two clean gloves. Do not forget the gloves."

I realized that Amina's constant warnings signalled a problem and I felt that the hospital should have notified us how many of the children were infected.

"Amina, these positive results should not be kept secret. Shouldn't we tell someone?" I asked.

She avoided my question.

"A year ago we had a child with AIDS from Chad," she told me. "It is not easy to infect the children. You worry unnecessarily."

Despite my misgivings, the children were kept together, regardless of whether they were healthy or infected with HIV. Everyone continued to work as before and the Filipino women continued re-using syringes. How many children were infected and whether or not this was as a result of the hospital staff's negligence, we will never know. We will also never know how many children were born HIV-positive.

The infected patients were eventually separated from the others. One hundred and eighty-three children were discovered to be HIV-positive. This was not just a problem—it was an epidemic. By now the parents of the children knew that the hospital was in crisis. They were ignorant about the causes of HIV and many resisted being tested, despite our encouragement. The father of one of the children even said that there was no way he could be HIV-positive, because he had never been in the children's hospital before.

The hospital became inundated with patients and a lot of strangers in white scrubs appeared. They were not doctors. They were elite police officers who had been commissioned by a man called Misheri to work undercover at the hospital. It never crossed my mind that they were police officers. We all thought they were either clerks or doctors. For months they hovered around the hospital wards, monitoring, observing and keeping records.

The noose around my neck was tightening with each passing day.

Lost

Emil and I only rented for a short while before we were offered a self-catering room in the hospital hostel at the beginning of 1999. Our daughter was to undergo an operation in Bulgaria and so plans had already been made for Emil to return while I continued working in Libya. Nevertheless, I was very happy about the new accommodation.

What I didn't know was that Djuma Misheri had ensured we would receive a room. He was the police colonel in charge of the strangers 'working' at the children's hospital. Why he assisted us, I have no idea, unless it was to keep me under observation while the police investigated the cause of the AIDS epidemic. At that stage I had seen him at the hospital but hadn't had any kind of communication with him. I had no idea that he was a police colonel in Tripoli, nor did I imagine what kind of influence he wielded. Emil had spoken with him on one occasion but we thought nothing of it when Misheri questioned him about why he planned to return to Bulgaria and how, shortly after Emil had told him about our dismal living arrangements, we were called into the Director's office to be offered better accommodation. We got approval to move into the hostel on 4 February 1999.

We stayed there only five days.

The 9th of February started out like any other work day. However, when we were getting ready to go home a man came to me and instructed: "Come quickly to the head nurse's office to get your passport." Several days before this we had been asked to hand in our passports—we assumed that this was standard practice with foreign employees.

A big group assembled in the head nurse's office—all Bulgarians, with the exception of two Polish ladies and one Filipino woman. This meeting had an ominous feel to it. We didn't recognize some of the

Libyan doctors, who, it turned out, were not doctors but senior police officers from Tripoli dressed in medical attire.

We waited for a long time for somebody to tell us what was happening and we grumbled among ourselves about the delay. Eventually one of our colleagues, a Polish lady lost her cool. "Come on, give us the passports and let us go. I have left the washing machine on at home and I need to get back."

We were told that they just needed to boot up the computer and they would then give us our documents. Time dragged on for what seemed forever. "I'm working the night shift—I have to go home first," our Filipino colleague protested. She was allowed to leave.

Finally it appeared that things were happening. First they called my colleague Maria to come to the surgery. After a few minutes they called the second nurse, me. I went into the office and—click! The door was locked from the outside. This did not seem right and I felt the first real flutters of anxiety. There was a Libyan man standing nearby and I asked him, "What's going on?"

"Go upstairs!" he ordered brusquely.

"But I need to get my passport," I objected.

"Your passport is upstairs," he told me.

He pushed me roughly toward the stairs. On the first landing I saw five or six plainclothes policemen. As I passed, two of them grabbed my hands and started questioning me.

"Who are you? Where do you work? What are you doing here?"

"I work in the infection unit. I'm here to get my passport!" I was shocked at the way they were manhandling me.

One of the policemen abruptly pulled my arms behind my back and tied my wrists with rope. I was terrified.

"What are you doing? What is going on here?" I cried.

"Shut up!" the policeman hissed, slapping my face.

I started shouting hysterically. Another policeman taped my mouth to silence me and then I was blindfolded. The brutality was so unexpected. I couldn't comprehend why they were treating me like this. We walked downstairs and out the building. They opened a door and shoved me into some kind of room. I couldn't work out where I was. I found a bench on which to sit. Every four or five minutes I heard the door opening and the sound of people being pushed into the room. Gradually I realized that I was in a truck or some kind of vehicle.

I couldn't see anything or mutter a sound, so I relied on my hearing. At one time I heard someone screaming hysterically, "No! No!" It was the voice of one of my colleagues, Valentina Siropulo. Her cries horrified me. I also heard a voice that I would get to know so well in the coming months—the voice of Djuma Misheri. I heard him tell Valentina to not worry, but then he instructed the policemen in Arabic: "Those who don't obey ... beat them."

I will never forget that voice. It's reminiscent of a dog barking. I also heard muffled screams and those whose mouths were not taped were yelling for help; their voices filling the air. I heard a Polish woman cry out: "If you touch us I will call the government in Poland. We will call the Pope and you will cry for your mother!" The Polish nurses had not been told to collect their passports but were still brought to the truck.

Meanwhile, my husband had been waiting for me to come home. He went to the dorm to ask our ex-roommate Nasya Nenova if she had seen me. She hadn't. He then went to look for the Filipino women and discovered that none of them were at work. Together they headed to the hospital. This decision was to be disastrous for Nasya, who had accompanied Emil because she had forgotten her keys at work. When she arrived she was informed that she needed to 'get her passport'. Very soon she found herself blindfolded and gagged with the rest of us.

Emil was taken to the registry and told to wait there. The windows had been painted. He realized that something was going on and peeled the paint off the windows with a key so that he could see what was happening outside. He had no idea that dozens of women were being kidnapped from the hospital at that moment, including me. He paced backwards and forwards, waiting for some kind of explanation regarding my whereabouts.

"What is he doing here?" an irate policeman shouted, spotting Emil in the registry room. The man's colleague—whom Emil had done some house repair work for—replied that he was there for a check-up. This man effectively saved Emil from being taken with the rest of us.

Emil never managed to find me.

When the policemen realized that he was Bulgarian, they locked him in a toilet, where he stayed until 3am until a Libyan cleaner released him. Inside the cubicle he overheard a policeman talking and learned that some of the staff had been arrested and that their bus was heading for Tripoli. He had no idea whether I was on this bus.

He searched for me at all the police stations and slowly came to the conclusion that I was one of the missing hospital staff. Nobody would explain to him what had happened and most people feigned ignorance.

While Emil frantically questioned hospital staff and local authorities in Benghazi, we were en route to Tripoli ...

ॐ ॐ ॐ

The truck lurched to a halt frequently. We sat blindfolded and gagged for hours, waiting to see what would happen. The truck returned to the hospital to collect others, including Nasya. They also picked up a Bulgarian woman I didn't know. When she was pushed into the truck I asked her who she was.

"My name is Kristiyana," she told me.

"What are you doing here?"

"I don't know. Who are you?" she asked.

"We are nurses at the children's hospital."

After several hours we stopped and our captors allowed us to remove our blindfolds for a few minutes so that we could go to the toilet in some roadside restaurant. Any thoughts of escape were laughable. It was a wasteland—nothing but desert surrounded us. Finally able to see, I took stock of my fellow prisoners. I knew all the faces with the exception of Kristiyana's. I wondered who she was and, for an instant, what she had done. I quickly concluded that she had probably done nothing wrong. I couldn't understand why we were all being subjected to such cruelty.

While at this dusty roadside restaurant I saw a policeman open a suitcase that had many passports inside, which I assumed were ours. I noted there was a sub-machine gun on the front seat of the truck. We were surrounded by dozens of policemen with guns. So when they instructed us to keep quiet, we instinctively obeyed.

At a quarter to six the following morning, we were 'escorted' into Sharon Nasser Police Station in the Libyan capital. I wasn't to leave here for a year and two months.

Seventeen women—sixteen nurses from the children's hospital in Benghazi and Kristiyana—were placed in a cell with a few mattresses and four blankets. We were all very confused and stressed; obviously none of us had any idea what was happening. I overheard a policeman telling one of the women that he might be the one interrogating us in connection with the AIDS epidemic at the hospital. Djuma Misheri's bizarre comments in the bus now seemed to make sense. He had said that a bomb at the Benghazi Hospital would be a good solution to the AIDS problem. He had also said that he would accommodate us in a 'five-star hotel'.

Our new acquaintance, Kristiyana, finally spoke. It turned out that she was also a nurse that worked in Benghazi, but at another hospital. We couldn't understand why she was included in our group—her hospital had no connection with ours and didn't have an AIDS epidemic that we were aware of. We could only surmise that she was here because she was Bulgarian.

At about 11am Kristiyana was taken from the cell. She was absent for the rest of the day and most of the night. They brought her back at a quarter to six the next morning and almost immediately transferred her to another cell.

Nasya Nenova was then called. She was also gone for a long time, almost eighteen hours. We agonized about these disappearances and the lack of information. We begged a policewoman to tell us where Nasya was. "She is with the *mudir* [the boss], drinking coffee," she said. This answer did not reassure us at all.

She was eventually brought back and put in a separate cell. We could see her through cracks in the wall as she passed in the corridor. Nasya was struggling to walk.

When the policemen took us out to use the bathroom we walked past her cell. Some of us whispered to her in Bulgarian.

"Did they beat you? Just say yes or no."

"Yes," she said with effort. "Are you all okay?"

The police officers yelled at us not to talk and pushed us along the corridor. We were terrified—if Nasya was asking such a question, she must have been severely hurt. We later found out that Nasya's torture was mild compared to what would happen to some of us. They had tied her up and given her an *a blanco* beating, which entails the recipient sitting on the ground with their arms between their legs and with their hands tied to a pole. They are then hung upside down by their feet like a butcher's carcass and are bludgeoned until they pass out.

The Libyans' interrogations didn't seem to follow any particular pattern. We sat in our cell wondering who would be next. Valentina Siropulo was called out two or three times and then brought back to our cell. They had asked her some general questions—when she had arrived in Libya, where she worked—without any violence or torture. We had no communication with Kristiyana and Nasya.

Despite the fear of retribution, Galya constantly urged the police to allow us access to a Bulgarian ambassador or representative. Djuma Misheri gathered us together and broke the news: "This is Libya, not Bulgaria; there is no ambassador for you."

On the fourth day the police rounded up Maria, Kristiyana, Valentina, Snezhana and myself and moved us to another cell. They started calling the rest of the women from the large cell, in groups of four or five at a time. None of them said anything when they returned except for Sevda, who was also from Byala Slatina. As she passed my cell she said: "Valya, Valya, I am very sorry for you, but do not fear. The interrogation went quickly and easily."

I didn't pay attention to the first part of her sentence. Only her words 'quickly and easily' registered. While we were in prison I gave a lot of thought to the first part of her sentence. I didn't understand that she had an inkling of what was to come. In a documentary that I watched years later, Sevda said that she saw Djuma Misheri putting away photographs of Nasya, Snezhana, Kristiyana and me. I believe that she and perhaps some of the other detained women may have 'sacrificed' us to save themselves.

The next day Sevda was released. I kept reassuring myself that the interrogation would be relatively painless.

The future proved me wrong.

The Red Carpet

Sevda's words had calmed me down. I told Valentina and Snezhana: "Relax! Obviously this isn't serious." My worries melted away—apparently there was some confusion and they would soon release us too. We must have been mistakenly imprisoned, I thought. I was an optimist.

Watching through our cell bars one day, Snezhana suddenly exclaimed, "They're taking them out!"

"Taking who out?" I asked her.

"Everyone."

I stood up, pushed my head through the bars and saw how almost all of the other Bulgarians were quietly leaving with a bag or two of luggage. None of them looked back at our cell or came to tell us anything.

There were no guards to ask what was happening and why seven of us were still detained. Valentina, Snezhana and I were in one cell and Nasya and Kristiyana were kept in separate cells after they returned from their brutal interrogations. In the original holding cell there were only two women left, Kalina and Maria. Kalina had been brought by military helicopter after everyone else. When we were being loaded into the bus, she had been away somewhere with her Maltese boyfriend. Colonel Djuma Misheri himself had 'captured' her.

Shortly after everybody had left Valentina, Snezhana and I were moved back to the big cell and Kalina was placed in our cell. A strange silence settled over us. I was frightened. I have always acted tough, but now I started to cry. Eventually I calmed down and rationalized that there was nothing to fear. So far, of the three of us, only Valentina had been questioned and none of us had been mistreated. In fact, it seemed as though the police had forgotten about us.

Our jailer was called Salma and she was our only link to the outside world. She asked us questions about ourselves and occasionally brought us food or took us to the toilet. We tried to worm information from her about our two colleagues who had been put in isolation cells, but she wouldn't tell us anything.

One day Nasya passed our cell and whispered in a hoarse voice, "Are you alive in there?"

We wanted to ask her a million questions. "Are you alright?", "What have they done to you?", "What's going on?" we asked, our questions spilling out in a flurry.

"My eye hurts," she replied.

We learned from Salma that she was not well and that they had called for a doctor.

A week passed. And then it came. The day I will never forget ...

On 23 February I had my first interrogation. A guard blindfolded me, covered me with a sheet and then pushed me inside a car. I didn't have the slightest idea where we were going and all my attempts to find out were met by stony silence. With a sinking feeling, I acknowledged that something sinister was probably planned for me.

The car stopped at last. Unknown hands pushed me up some stairs, somewhere ... We reached a corridor and they leaned me against the wall. They took the sheet away, but left the blindfold on. I could see a red carpet through a small slit in the blindfold. I saw a man's foot. It belonged to the interpreter, who barked at me.

"Do you know why you are here?"

"I don't know."

"What do you mean you don't know?" he snarled.

"I do not know why I'm here!"

"Are you sure that you don't know?" he insisted.

"Yes," I answered truthfully.

"You do know. Why are you here? Why are you here?" he repeated.

He asked me five more times. How was I supposed to answer when I didn't have the slightest idea why all this was happening?

"Do you know anything about the AIDS?" he asked.

"I don't know what you're talking about," I told him.

He sighed loudly. A moment later rough hands grabbed me again. They put me in a room and I could only see my feet as we walked on the red carpet. I caught a glimpse of some chairs and desks and a lot of people. They sat me down on a chair. The interrogation continued.

"What is your name?", "What are your mother and father called? "Where have you worked before?" "Why are you in Libya?"

I answered the questions quickly and accurately. I was not afraid, despite the blindfold. The questions were mundane and repetitive. The interview then changed tack.

"What do you know about AIDS?"

"I don't know anything; I don't know what you're talking about."

"Why don't you know about it?" a man shouted.

I heard someone address one of the interrogators as Mustafa and whisper something to him that I could not understand. He came closer to me. I felt his breath on my face. I could basically make out his outline because the blindfold was made of a thin material and its edges had frayed. Mustafa took a lighter and lit a loose thread. Then another. I tensed when I smelt the burning material. I heard a voice cry out, "*Haram*, Mustafa! That's a sin, Mustafa. Don't!"

"Tell me about AIDS. What do you know?" he tried again. I didn't answer him. They dragged me to the hallway. Then it started. They made me sit down and tied my hands and ankles with a rope, then hung me upside down by my legs. My experience with the *a blanco* beating had begun.

One of the interrogators pulled out a thick black cable and lashed me.

The first blow cut through my heels with a pain I had never experienced. I was being whipped!

All the while my interrogator shrieked at me, "Tell us about AIDS!"

"I don't know anything!"

"AIDS!"

"I don't know about it."

"AIDS, you idiot!"

I tried to twist my body to deflect each blow to my feet. It hurt terribly. Every few seconds I felt excruciating pain ... I don't remember how many times my feet were whipped. I didn't even have the strength to scream. I fainted and they took me down. When I came to I was hung up again and the sadistic lashing continued. About ten men took turns whipping me and they were relentless. When one got tired, the next immediately took over. I did not cry, I did not moan. Somehow I resigned myself to the thought that I was going to die. I can't explain this feeling. I thought it could get no worse. I fainted again. I heard, "Collapsed, collapsed! She has fainted, she has fainted!"

They threw water on my face. Still hanging, I moved a little. The blows started again. "Tell us everything. What do you know about AIDS?"

The pain had numbed my wits. I could not speak. At some stage— maybe after fifty, one hundred, five hundred lashes later—the cable finally dropped to the ground. The interpreter said to the room at large: "So you don't want to talk. Then we'll give you some scorpions ..."

A few seconds later I felt something crawling on my face. I began squirming in terror. From beneath the blindfold I saw something black scuttling across my skin toward my eyes. The pain and fear overwhelmed me and I passed out again.

When I regained consciousness, I was sprawled out on the red carpet. I clearly saw the faces of the monsters who had tortured me. They threw water over me again. Mustafa shouted, "Coma, coma" and his accomplice said in Arabic, "Bring the electricity, bring the electricity!" I desperately thought that death by electrocution would be a welcome release. I was soaking wet. Heavy slaps rained down on my face and coarse voices summoned me to return to the nightmare: "Valya, Valya, Valya, VALYA!" They made me sit up. My feet were purple from the blows and the pain was indescribable. They then helped me stand and dragged me to a chair. A man asked me, "Do you want a cigarette?" He gave me one, but I was shaking so much that I couldn't put it to my lips.

They lifted up my shirt. More scorpions were applied. I wondered why I was still alive; why they hadn't stung me. Later I found out that they were in fact huge black beetles.

I had totally surrendered. I was ready to die.

"How did the AIDS infection happen?" Mustafa asked me.

"AIDS can be transmitted by blood transfusion or sex." I did not understand what they were actually asking me or what they wanted to hear.

"How were the children at the hospital infected?"

"The children … I don't know," I stammered.

"You do know. How can you not know?" he pressed.

"What do you want from me?" I shouted.

"We want you to tell us about the AIDS!"

The 'scorpions' were crawling around my navel and were on my face. They hung me up again.

"You'll stay like that all night until you tell us," the interpreter yelled at me.

They kept their promise. All night I hung there, upside down with my hands tied and my eyes blindfolded. The red carpet spread out underneath me.

"Tell me what you know about AIDS in the hospital?"

"I don't know anything!"

"Tell us about Kristiyana."

"I don't know her; I saw her for the first time in the prison."

"Tell us about AIDS! Admit you know about Kristiyana! When did you meet her?"

"Here, in prison."

"This is not true. Tell us about Kristiyana. Tell us about AIDS!"

"I don't know anything. I don't know her."

"Bullshit, you don't know her. She is a prostitute with money!"

"I don't know her. I saw her for the first time in the cell before you took her away. We have only been together for a couple of hours!"

"No, she is a prostitute and you know her. She gave you money! Tell us about Kristiyana. Confess about the AIDS."

Kristiyana, Kristiyana. Some of the arrested women had worked with her in surgery at another hospital but I had never met her. My interrogators kept insisting that I had told them about her. This continued all night long. A night in which every minute felt like an hour. A night in which every painful lashing made me want to die. A night in which I never understood what they wanted to hear from me. I have no recollection of when they took me down.

When we got back to the prison I was thrown into a new cell, cell number five. While I was being dragged along the corridor, I heard either Nasya or Snezhana call out to me: "Valya! Are you coming back?"

"They've beaten me like a dog," I muttered before a blow to my head put an end to any further communication.

I came to in a dark, narrow, nightmarish cell. I had been beaten, was wet, barefoot and could not walk. In fact, I couldn't even stand. Salma, our jailer, tossed some slippers at me and left me lying on the ground.

"Get up," she instructed.

"I can't," I told her matter-of-factly, looking up at her from the floor.

"Get up," she said again.

"I can't stand on my feet," I explained.

"Ha ha," she cackled. "You really can't. Good gracious, they really thrashed you hard!"

I got cold in the night and Salma threw a blanket over my soaking wet clothes. I wanted to go to the bathroom but she made me use a bucket instead. I just lay there; I don't know for how many days. Every single movement I made was agonizing. How easy it is to write about it now, but how hard it was to endure. Time had no meaning. I lay in the cell, aware only of the filth, pain and terror. I never imagined I would experience something so horrific. I didn't know then that the nightmare was only just beginning.

After several days I heard that the others were being taken somewhere. I learned from Salma that there was to be a meeting with Lyudmil Spassov, a Bulgarian envoy and the future ambassador in Tripoli. The meeting was to be held in Diashabi. I heard guards talking in Arabic about us: "The beaten? No. Only the others can go!" The 'beaten' referred to Nasya, who had been tortured first, and to myself. I was literally one huge bruise. I wanted to peep through the bars when they started taking the prisoners out, but my injuries made it difficult for me to hoist myself up from the floor.

After the others had left, a policeman offered me a cigarette—a small gesture of kindness. Salma had gone to the meeting and he was now responsible for Nasya and me.

When he wasn't looking, I tried to see Nasya through a crack in the wall. I wanted to find out whether she was alright in her adjacent cell. We had been forbidden from speaking to one another, but I didn't care about being caught and punished because I was sure I would soon die sanyway. She looked broken. She was huddled in a corner and she didn't answer me when I called her name.

Lyudmil Spassov was aware that seven Bulgarian nurses were still being detained. Since Nasya and I were not fit to attend the meeting, the Libyans had to make up the requisite numbers. A Bulgarian mother and daughter who were detained at another prison served as perfect substitutes. They were threatened that if they said a word they would suffer for it. I don't know what the detainees could and did say at the meeting, but Bulgaria's envoy returned from it very calm and reassured that everything was fine. My husband managed to contact him and he demanded to know where I was. Spassov told him that, "There is nothing to worry about; your wife has gone to Benghazi. She is already travelling with the rest of the women who were released."

Nasya's colleagues showed Lyudmil a picture of her and asked whether he had seen her at the meeting. He affirmed that he had when in truth he could not possibly have seen her, because at that time she was bloodied and bruised in her cell a few metres away from me. I don't know why he behaved as he did—whether it was gross negligence, or whether he had been misled somehow—but he was absolutely irresponsible. In front of the Bulgarian journalists, who had begun to follow our case with interest, the man entrusted with the task of protecting us, conveyed the words of the Libyan Foreign Minister Omar al-Muntaser to the world.

"The detainees are in a good physical and mental state, their safety is not jeopardized and their rights are guaranteed by the law. Most detained Bulgarian nationals have already been released and the release of the others will happen when the preliminary trial is over, provided there is an element of openness and goodwill. The trial will be conducted with absolute transparency, fairness and impartiality, without any bias and discrimination against the accused, whatever their nationality."

He added: "They are doing well; they are sleeping on white sheets."

My 'sheet' was the floor of cell number five.

After several hours Kristiyana, Snezhana, Maria, Valentina and Kalina came back to the prison. Kristiyana was put in cell number four, right next to me. I waited until the guard was out of earshot and then began banging on her wall.

"Kristiyana, can you hear me? Where have you been?"

"We were in an office. We met ... I don't know who. They said they had found blood infected with AIDS at my house. My husband was at work ... I don't know what is happening, what they planted. I didn't understand anything."

Well, she was about to understand. Only a few hours later they took her away—for a walk on the red carpet. There she experienced her own nightmare. She was hung from a door for hours and they used dogs to frighten her. They accused her of having improper sexual relations with Ashraf, a young doctor from the children's hospital. Ashraf was imprisoned elsewhere and was tortured with electric cables attached to his penis before being raped. One can't deny that the Libyan authorities have a wide and persuasive arsenal of 'truth-inspiring' weapons. We were yet to experience them all.

Kristiyana was severely beaten. When she was returned to her cell she was sobbing and could not speak of what had happened.

Several days later, Maria and Kalina were also questioned and then released. They were not on the receiving end of any beatings or torture techniques. I learned of their release by eavesdropping on Salma's conversation with another guard.

There were only five of us left. Nasya and I were left to recover from our interrogations, while Kristiyana was tortured on a daily basis. Snezhana and Valentina had not been questioned yet. We didn't know each other, but we would forever be bound to one another because of our shared experiences.

My 'Accomplices'

I had vaguely known Valentina Siropulo and Nasya Nenova before our arrest. We had travelled to Libya together in 1998 and Emil and I had lived in an apartment with Nasya for a short time. We were all contracted by the children's hospital in Benghazi but worked in different units. As such, I didn't know either of them very well.

Perhaps we should have realized that Libya was not a particularly safe place for foreign medical personnel and that turbulent times lay ahead. At the end of 1998 several nurses were taken into police custody, including Snezhana. They were all foreigners—Filipino, Polish, Hungarian and Bulgarian. They were questioned about the first reported case of a child dying of AIDS at the children's hospital.

I didn't think anything of it as nothing untoward seemed to have happened and they returned after a few days. The Hungarian nurse was released from the police station on the second day. Her country's ambassador had heard of her detention and immediately took action. The Filipino and Polish ambassadors quickly followed suit. The Bulgarian nurses remained at the police station, with no one to intercede on their behalf. Once they had been released, a man from the company that had found us employment popped in to the hospital to see what had happened. I was the only Bulgarian on shift and he tried to make light of the situation.

"Well, I heard the police freed our nurses. This is nothing, right? Just a misunderstanding."

"No, it is very serious," I scolded him. I did not care for his flippant attitude.

"Well, I'll find them and ask what happened."

He never looked for them and he never met them. The Bulgarian

Embassy paid little attention to the incident and never informed the Bulgarian ambassador about it. Snezhana later told me that there had been no 'evidence' linking any of the nurses to the AIDS outbreak and that the prosecutor of Benghazi had said, "This is an old problem in Benghazi. We have known about the infection for three years already."

This was the Libyans' first attempt to find a foreign scapegoat to pin the AIDS epidemic on. The Filipino nurses were the most likely suspects because their work practices were shoddy, but their country interceded on their behalf. The Bulgarian nurses, on the other hand, had nobody to represent them and so a plan was hatched: Bulgarians could be targeted with no diplomatic repercussions.

At the beginning of 1999, just a few weeks after the 'trial' interrogation, Bulgarian nurses were rounded up in their droves from the children's hospital. The police intended to ambush Kristiyana Vulcheva at her home but she was not in. When she finally returned from the market, they stopped her and asked her if she had a *maharma*, a headscarf. They then told her to put it on and to get her things because they were taking her for 'a brief check-up'.

The police planted bags of blood at her home, which they later claimed were HIV-positive. On the basis of this fabricated evidence, Kristiyana would later be branded the ringleader of the HIV outbreak at the children's hospital, a malicious woman who ordered her fellow Bulgarian nurses to infect the children. In reality, she was a fun-loving, ordinary woman who enjoyed doing housework and organizing parties. She didn't mince her words and had quite probably made enemies during her time in Libya.

Three men are involved in this story of unjust persecution—Ashraf al-Hadjudj, Zdravko Georgiev and Smilyan Tachev. I first met Ashraf al-Hadjudj in the children's section, where he was an intern. This young Palestinian trainee impressed me because, unlike the other doctors with grubby stethoscopes and stained lab coats, he always took great care to look professional and clean. On some night shifts we happened to drink coffee together—along with other doctors and nurses from the four units of the children's floor. I remember chatting with him once or twice. The Libyans regarded him as a man with no state to call home and I can only guess that he became embroiled in our drama because of this. It seems as though the police only detained people from countries that didn't care for its citizens abroad ... or those whose home countries were undergoing political upheaval and had more important problems than securing the release of detained expatriates. Ashraf was arrested ten days before us, on 29 January 1999, and was then moved to Tripoli. From that moment on his fate was inextricably bound with ours.

Zdravko Georgiev was married to Kristiyana. When she was taken away he alerted the Bulgarian Consulate. His pleas fell on deaf ears. Ironically, he was arrested in front of its gates. Kristiyana desperately tried to find out whether her husband had been implicated when she went to the meeting with Lyudmil Spassov and he had fobbed her off. That same evening, however, while they were leading her away to be interrogated, she saw his bag and began to suspect that they had detained him as well.

Smilyan Tachev, a Bulgarian medical technician, was the last to join us at the Sharon Nasser Police Station. He arrived on 8 March, several days after I was first tortured. I immediately noticed his trainers were embossed with 'Benghazi', but I didn't know that he had been accused of being an accomplice.

Why had he been arrested? Because he featured in many of the photographs seized from Kristiyana's home. Smilyan had met Kristiyana when he was helping one of her colleague's daughters with her physics studies. Later, he and Kristiyana lived in the same house. The rest of us didn't know him.

Smilyan was one of the few people who had gone looking for us after we mysteriously disappeared. The police didn't like that so when they discovered Kristiyana's photo albums, his fate was sealed. He was accused of manufacturing the virus which infected the children in our hospital. He was initially told that he would be released. Djuma Misheri then went above the prosecutor's head and insisted that he must be questioned further. He wasn't even provided with an interpreter during his interrogation. Instead, a Libyan man who knew only a spattering of Bulgarian tried to translate what Smilyan was saying.

Smilyan's challenge in prison was immense—he was kept in isolation for six months. When they interrogated him in a room adjacent to my cell, he wasn't physically tortured. That isn't to say that he wasn't mistreated; they mentally crushed him. The only place he went out to was the toilet. Sometimes, however, they 'forgot' him and tossed him cardboard boxes to use. Once they didn't let him out for four days. Another time they made him wash with water that dozens of prisoners had spat in. He was made to wash his clothes himself and when they were still drying, our jailer, Salma, would not give him other clothes to wear to the bathroom. She gave him an old raincoat instead. I didn't know this person, but I wept like a child seeing what he was put through.

One day they took him outside and he managed to secretly steal a rope. He waited till there was nobody around and then showed it to me through a crack in the wall.

"Let's hang ourselves," he said. He meant it. He told me that the guards had been bringing him to listen to us when we were being tortured.

"Why hang ourselves and give them an excuse to say that we were guilty of something we had nothing to do with?" I replied.

As far as I was concerned, they could kill me but I would never voluntarily end my own life. I managed to talk him out of it and got him to give me the rope. I showed the rope to Salma and she took it away.

During the six months that he was imprisoned I learned to appreciate what a good-natured man he was. He was very intelligent and had completed two masters degrees. He was also a vegetarian. When Salma prepared our sandwiches, she used peppers or parsley that were half-rotten. She would sometimes throw the vegetables out and Smilyan would retrieve them from the bin. Why waste good vitamins, he reasoned.

It was a mystery why they had detained us five women together with Ashraf, Zdravko and Smilyan. I think it was just down to bad luck. We had apparently drawn the short straws.

Smilyan was released in August and no reason was given.

It never crossed my mind that any of us were guilty. The Libyans were not interested in looking for the real culprits. They were looking for scapegoats so that they could conceal their hospital's negligence. They did not care whose lives they destroyed. We were paying for somebody else's sins. We had been targeted because we were foreigners who were not protected by our consulates. We didn't even know each other, but this didn't stop the Libyan authorities from declaring to the world that we had jointly orchestrated a monstrous crime.

The Hell in Me

My feet and legs were still bruised seven days after my interrogation. Deep down I knew that more torture was in the offing as I hadn't told them what they wanted to hear. I lay in my cell, willing my body to heal. I was offered no medicine.

My next interrogation happened during the daytime. Again they drove me to the facility blindfolded. On the way to the interrogation room I heard a man screaming with pain and other men yelling at him. It was Ashraf, although I didn't realize that at the time. I could hear the sound of grinding metal and then the unmistakable sounds of an *a blanco* beating. The man cried out, *"Alay,* Allah! In the name of the Lord! On the *rasa* [head] of my mother, I swear I do not know them."

"If you don't want to die, tell us," Djuma Misheri bellowed. "Admit it! Say 'I know them'."

Ashraf vehemently swore that he didn't know whoever they were referring to. I soon learned that they were torturing him to confess that he knew us, the Bulgarian nurses.

The guards stationed me outside the room he was in so that I could listen. I made out that they were showing him our passports.

"This is Snezhana. This is Valentina. This is Kristiyana. This is Valya. This is Nasya," a man shouted. "You know them. Admit it. Say you were with them, that you've worked with them. We know everything ... Say it!"

He didn't know us. How could he? We may have seen each other in the hospital and possibly have smoked cigarettes in each other's company, but there were lots of Bulgarian nurses working there and we had done nothing to stand out. Besides, these are tiny instances that one forgets.

Suddenly it was my turn to identify my 'accomplices'.

"Admit it or we'll hang you. We'll hang you today, you know," a man snarled at me, pointing at a scary-looking gallows.

"What am I to admit? I don't know anything," I pleaded.

They didn't hang me but beat me severely that day ... and almost every day afterwards. They were experts in the art of torture and they frequently alternated techniques—sometimes beating me, electrocuting me or setting dogs on me. I suffered excruciating pain in almost every part of my body. All these agonizing experiences merged. Hour after hour, day after day, new horrors were inflicted one after another. Eventually one loses a sense of time, place, of everything. And most of all the will to live.

Between interrogations they would bring us back to the police station. Our driver was named Djuma Moloto. When he came to collect us from our cells I knew that pain was just around the corner—that eight or nine bloodthirsty men would thrash me to within an inch of my life and twenty more would watch.

Djuma was present when we were tortured, but didn't torture me himself. In other circumstances, I would probably think him a decent man. When he returned my bruised and bloody body to my cell, he would bring me water. Sometimes milk or cigarettes. Once when driving me back to the police station, he tried to cheer me up, joking: "Hey, Valya. With those pretty green eyes of yours, when everything is over I want you to give birth to my children." I don't think he meant to offend me.

I desperately wanted to communicate with the others. Salma made me mop the floor when I could barely walk, so I used this to my advantage, whispering to my colleagues as I passed their cells.

"Where is Nasya?" they asked me.

"I don't know," I said.

"Snezhana is very sick," they told me.

"I was thrashed," I heard one of the women say.

When I was next 'thrashed', it was one of the most brutal sessions yet. It started off as it typically did.

"Tell us what you know," my interrogator insisted.

"I don't know anything. I can confess nothing. Nothing happened," I said.

"Well, now we'll see what you don't know. You will confess it all. Here he is; he knows," a man said, taking off my blindfold.

Ashraf was brought into the room. There was almost nothing left of him. He was a skeleton; he didn't even look like a man. His face was unshaven and grey.

At first I didn't recognize him. In the next few seconds I realized that we worked at the same hospital.

"You know this guy?" I was asked.

"No," I told them.

"Well, he knows you. You drank coffee together. Tell her, *maas*! Tell her, scum," he hissed at Ashraf.

"One night in the hospital I saw how she infected a child with AIDS," Ashraf said, looking at the floor.

I was in shock. "Liar! That's a lie. You've just made that up," I burst out.

Djuma Misheri was livid. He started beating Ashraf because he hadn't been convincing and I was grabbed by the throat. A man began to strangle me. I saw other men pointing at the gallows. The hands tightened around my throat and yet again I thought that I would die. I didn't appreciate that they needed me alive. Shortly before I lost consciousness, Adel, the clerk who was keeping shorthand notes of the questioning, shouted that one of the superiors was coming and that they must stop. The man let me go.

I was taken to another room. My blindfold was taken off. I could see my tormentors—animals—about ten of them. They took turns questioning me. A policeman pushed me into a chair. I was at one side of the desk and the clerk was on the other, recording everything.

"Tell us everything you know!"

"I do not know anything," I cried.

Djuma Moloto then told me that it would all be over if I would only confess.

"But I do not know anything," I protested. Looking him squarely in the eyes, I said as calmly as I could, "I don't know anything."

"It's true; you can tell by her eyes that she is not lying," he said to the others.

Huge mistake. Another man approached, taking a puff of his cigarette.

"Wow, who took off her blindfold?" he addressed the room at large. "Now we're going to have to remove her eyes if they show that she's not lying."

He took the cigarette out of his mouth and menacingly held it in front of my face. If he put it in my eye he would blind me forever ...

∻ ∻ ∻

The burning cigarette butt moved toward my left eye with frightening speed. Even after everything I had been through, I had never felt such terror. It all happened in seconds. Djuma Moloto screamed and knocked the man's hand away at the last possible moment. The cigarette was subsequently extinguished on the side of my head, where I still have a scar today.

"It's a sin!" I heard someone else cry.

The policeman flew into a fit of rage and a colleague pushed him away from me. Everybody started screaming in Arabic. I no longer understood what they were saying. I could only make out a few phrases: "You go", "You stay", "Why isn't she blindfolded?", "Blindfold her". They turned their backs to me. They didn't want me to see who was behind this madness, especially if I was innocent.

Then the torture started. A man grabbed a heavy book and started hitting me all over my body. He hit me hard, screaming as he did so. He banged my head with the book again and again. Then the man who had almost blinded me grabbed a metal rod and started beating my hands with it. The non-stop hysteria and incredible pain continued all night and the next day my hands bore witness to the terrors I had endured. They were bruised deep blue and covered with burst veins.

The following few days and nights were one never-ending nightmare. You've heard the expression 'black and blue'. Well, I was a walking—no, hobbling—example. There wasn't a single millimetre of my body that was not a shade of black or blue. On my birthday, March 22 1999, I received a special gift from the policemen—they beat me all day long, whipping and kicking me. In the evening the 'gifts' continued in the jail as well. They took us all out of the cells, blindfolded us, and told us to raise our hands and stand on one foot. We did that for three days, changing foot once a day. At some point we each succumbed to weakness and fatigue, lowering a leg or arm. Every time someone faltered, their arm or leg was lashed with a hose.

Like me, Kristiyana was blue-black from her fingertips to her toes. She cried all the time. Valentina was also not in a good state. During the bizarre 'Simon says' routine, she had been brutally whipped with the hose when she couldn't continue standing on her numb leg and had torn a muscle. Knowing this, Salma made her jump around in the cell. She broke her ankle and, in an act of small mercy, the authorities allowed her to receive medical treatment.

Of all the tortures I endured, it was the dogs that truly terrified me.

I wasn't ever actually attacked, but the fear was overwhelming. I was taken to a cell which housed several trained German Shepherds. There was a large opening in the middle of one wall. Five or six policemen were gathered there to assist with my questioning. One of them stood behind me, pinning my arms behind my back. He started asking me the usual questions. I didn't answer him. He pushed me toward the dogs and they started barking savagely. He would pull me back and then push me forward, over and over, each time edging me closer to their snapping jaws. At first I wasn't really afraid of the animals. I thought that the dogs would know I was innocent and a good person and wouldn't do anything to me.

I was then beaten viciously and when I fell to the ground, my tormentors lifted me up and made me squat on my haunches and 'duck-walk' around the corridors. I physically couldn't. So they set a snarling dog behind me to improve my cooperation. It barked and jumped, straining against its lead, catching some of my hair in its teeth. It was a terrible, terrible thing to feel its hot breath on my neck and be unable to do anything about it. Thankfully, I wasn't bitten. Later, however, after our session had ended, Salma showed me a 'real' interrogation with dogs. The victim was a Libyan man and he was blindfolded. One of his hands was cuffed to a staircase and he was hanging from it. A policeman pointed out to the dog where it should bite.

"Now, here," he pointed at the man's trousers. The dog immediately tore into his leg.

"Come on, here now," he said again and with that the torn clothing fell to the ground.

The man was crying, swearing that he was innocent. The officer then ordered the dog to gently 'skin him' with its teeth. The dog barked incessantly at the victim and again and again the policeman would give orders and indicate with a stick where the dog should bite. The man screamed in terror, but wouldn't 'confess'. The policeman's stick kept touching other parts of his body and the dog would rip into his flesh. Hands, legs, arms and torso were mutilated. The Libyan was totally covered in blood. I became very scared and realized what could happen if they really turned the dogs on me. Apparently, my tormentors had only ordered the dog to bite my hair.

ॐ ॐ ॐ

One day they dragged me to a new place, a kind of bunker. Djuma Misheri himself questioned me. He went on and on about the AIDS virus I had allegedly infected the children with.

"Where did you get the virus from?" he demanded.

"I do not know what you mean," I said.

"Why do you not know?"

"I don't know anything."

"You'll remember now," he threatened.

They tied my hands with a cable. It was attached to two fingers of my left hand and to two fingers of the right.

"Go!" Misheri ordered.

Have you ever been shocked by an electric fence? If you have, you'll know what it feels like to have a current surge through your body, its sheer power knocking you to the ground. Now imagine that feeling multiplied by a thousand and lasting not just a second, but endless minutes. Not just in one spot either, but all over your body. This was my first experience of electrical torture. It seared every bit of me with a kind of pain that is almost impossible to describe. It was as though they were tearing me to pieces while millions of knives stabbed me. I grew faint and was losing consciousness. Djuma was very careful to keep me awake.

"Stop, stop. Turn it down," he said. "I want her alive."

They gave me a short break so that I could recover. All too soon, the torture resumed. My whole body shook. I'm dying, I thought. It was paralyzing me, reaching my throat, choking me ... I couldn't take it anymore. I'M DYING! But no. They always stopped in time.

"Tell me about AIDS now," Misheri demanded.

"I don't know anything."

"Tell me everything," he said.

"I don't know anything," I maintained.

"Tell me at least one name."

"I don't know who did it."

"Say 'Kristiyana'."

"I don't know her."

"Say 'Ashraf'."

"I don't know him."

"You bitch!"

This type of interrogation became commonplace. I often collapsed and my heart stopped twice—the high-voltage current nearly killed me. I still have scars on my hands from where the cables were attached.

When the cable clamps could no longer grip my skin because it had become bloodied and torn, they attached the cables to my feet. The current coursing through my body felt as though wild beasts were eating me from inside. Once, Djuma Misheri put a live cable against my head. "If you don't speak now, you will die here," he said. The pain was unbearable.

He grew angry because the current had incapacitated my speach. Then Djuma instructed the men: "Tie her in the most painful way."

This time they connected the cables so that they ran diagonally across my body, with one cable attached to my left ankle and the other to my right hand. It was the worst form of torture yet and I was used as a human circuit board. The most agonizing pain blazed through my body and in that instant I believed I was in hell. I was in hell and the hell was in me.

I don't know how long it lasted but it felt like forever. After they took the cables off, they kicked me repeatedly and smashed my head against a steel cabinet. My whole body was stiff from the electrical torture and I couldn't move. I slumped to the ground as those miscreants pulled me by my hair and legs and dragged me across the floor to get my blood circulating.

I had forgotten who I was and where I was. My brain went into total shut-down. I couldn't remember simple things—my daughters' names, what bread was, why I was here. I wasn't sure if I was awake or asleep. I was dying a little more every single day while God watched it happen.

Valentina was nearly killed by one of the five electrical machines they used. She couldn't speak for several days. I don't know which one damaged her so badly—the one they rolled over your body or the cables that would pump pure pain. At the torture facility I listened to the shrieks of my comrades as they were electrocuted to within an inch of death.

I can't write about this anymore. I don't want to remember it. Even the most amoral or despicable person in this world does not deserve such punishment. And I hadn't done anything!

えええ

Djuma Misheri was persistent. I was stubborn. I was not going to confess to a crime which I had nothing to do with. I used all my strength— physical, mental and emotional—to survive. He always threatened me with even harsher forms of punishment.

"Tell me about AIDS. Have you forgotten already?" he sneered into my face.

"I don't know anything," I told him for the hundredth time.

"You do. You will remember. Give her the injection," he said, pointing at one of his henchmen.

They plunged the needle into the carotid artery behind my ear. It hurt. I didn't know what they were injecting me with—it crossed my mind that it might be HIV-positive blood. I lost consciousness and when I woke up, I was being spun on some kind of contraption. To this day I don't know if I imagined this. I plunged in and out of a dream state. It was a disgusting and disorientating sensation. I have a vague recollection of the questions and that Djuma Misheri told the interpreter: "Not in Arabic, not in Bulgarian. Speak to her in English."

"Who was the first child? What do you know about the AIDS?" the interpreter asked.

Then, "How did you pick the children?"

Followed by, "Did you know that Ashraf saw you?"

"How much money did you receive?" he pressed.

I now understood exactly what they expected me to tell them. They were accusing me, the other nurses and Ashraf of having deliberately infected the children at the hospital with AIDS. How Kristiyana was supposed to be involved in all this was not clear, given that she had never set foot in the hospital. However, they were determined to get answers that would inculpate us. I would not confess that I was a mass murderer, no matter how much pain I endured. If I was going to die, so be it.

They upped the intensity of the torture sessions, abruptly alternating between drugging me and electrocuting me. My mind was like a sieve. I barely remembered what happened after the injections. I can hazily recall being injected with 'ten cc' of something that was white as milk and a doctor who was angry because he was not allowed to give me something called *abokat* to put me to sleep. Once I woke up to find what I assumed was an interpreter standing next to me with a small dictaphone.

I remember being in an unfamiliar room with a mattress on a desk. I could hear the screams of the others in the distance. I was connected to IV drips and an oxygen bottle. I was teetering toward oblivion when I felt something that I can only describe as 'wind' moving through my body. It must have been the oxygen. I revived and needed to go to the bathroom. They brought me a piece of tubing to use instead. Then the IV drips were inserted again.

"Go to hell!" the interpreter hissed when I regained consciousness. I heard Nasya screaming hysterically and was then violently thrown onto a mattress.

After I had been injected several times, I couldn't tell day from night, truth from lie, fantasy from memory. Suicide crossed my mind in moments of weakness, but the thought of seeing my children again gave me strength.

Lies and Confessions

I lay in my cell recuperating after a vigorous bout of injection torture the day before. I could barely move. The stench of my own flesh permeated the air. I had an inhuman thirst. Djuma Moloto, the man who had saved me from losing my eye to a burning cigarette butt a few weeks earlier, brought a me glass of water. "Drink up, you're going with Salma," he said.

I was then given soap with which to wash myself. We were obviously going to a meeting of some sort.

The next thing I knew, I was being escorted out of the prison. I was bundled into a car and a guard gave me some shoes to put on. They would not have bothered if I was just going to the torture centre, would they? I begged for more water but was ignored. Cramps racked my body and I started vomiting out the car window. I was let out to get some fresh air. Then Smilyan, Snezhana and I were all loaded into the car. Valentina did not come with us as she still couldn't talk.

Snezhana cried the whole way there, hysterically weeping, "They will kill us," over and over. I tried to calm her down, but her wails just grew louder and more frantic. A policeman whipped his head around and glared angrily at us. He then spoke to the interpreter in a flurry of Arabic, gesticulating wildly. It was no surprise that the interpreter told us to shut up, or else face the wrath of Djuma Misheri. He also told us that we were meeting with Roumen Petrov, a diplomat at the Bulgarian Embassy. We thought that this was good news, despite the interpreter's warning: "You will not talk or complain at this meeting."

If it weren't for Nasya, this meeting would not have happened. After she 'confessed' to Djuma Misheri, she slit her wrists. She was rushed to hospital, where she screamed to anybody who would listen that they must "save the others, they are innocent too". She told our story to every nurse and doctor she came in contact with and explained how we were being tortured. Some of the Bulgarians she spoke with called the embassy. Finally, 'unofficial' information had reached the right people.

We entered the building where the meeting was to be held, full of hope. Nasya, Kristiyana and her husband Zdravko were already there. This was the first time I met Zdravko. He was thin, unshaven and looked like an old man. He seemed so different to how Kristiyana had described him. She too had not seen him until now and was shocked by how prison had aged him.

Our optimism was short-lived. Roumen Petrov seemed to not know or believe anything of what had happened to us in prison. He also didn't show any sympathy toward us. We were desperate for news of our loved ones and all he said to me was, "Your daughters say hello. They are fine." What had happened with the operation? What about Emil? Where was he? I thought. He was cool toward Nasya too, telling her: "Your relatives called. They said to tell you that we only have one life to live so don't try to take it away again. Everything will be okay."

"I hope it doesn't turn out that you were involved," he said. He didn't believe we hadn't done anything wrong!

"As I understand it, the examining magistrate is here. The investigation will go on for a while longer still," he added.

That was the level of support we received from our country. He proceeded to tell the Bulgarian authorities that we were in good shape.

Nasya had already admitted to her 'involvement' but the Libyan authorities wanted her to finger us as well. They tantalized her, promising instant release if she would implicate us.

"Say that they were also involved and you'll go home," Djuma Misheri coaxed.

"But I don't know it was them," Nasya replied.

"Say that you know it was them and you'll get off. Tomorrow you could be back in Benghazi."

Nasya and Ashraf were interrogated together. In front of Nasya, the police put a gun to his temple and forced him to recite his 'confession' in an effort to coerce Nasya to implicate us. Pitifully, when he was finished he looked at Djuma Misheri and asked, "Was that okay, sir?" Nasya resisted and they increased the intensity of her torture. By the end of the day, Nasya didn't know her name and thought perhaps she had done something that she later forgot.

Kristiyana and Ashraf then confessed. To make sure their stories corroborated, the police tortured them together. Terrified, they were hung by their arms from the windows, their muscles stretching and spasming as they dangled above the hard ground below. Every movement, voluntary or not, made them writhe with agony. They both signed tailor-made confessions thereafter.

They were made to rehearse their confessions, sometimes with guns to their heads. For every wrong answer or discrepancy, further torture ensued.

Snezhana was tortured the least. I am not sure why. She was a very frail-looking woman and perhaps they worried that they would kill her accidentally. Perhaps her faith saved her. She told the policemen that Mohammed appeared to her when she was being tortured.

Valentina, on the other hand, was offered no leniency. Once when they brought her back from the torture facility, I thought she was dead. She did not move for hours. I was very scared. When she did eventually come to, her eyes constantly moved as if following the pendulum of a clock—left, right, left, right—she couldn't control it and she couldn't stop. For the next few days she was like a breathing corpse. I washed and nursed her. I could see she was wasting away, body and mind.

The Libyans were livid that she wouldn't confess so they wired her tongue. She could not speak for two months afterwards. Another time, the voltage was so high that her resolve temporarily shattered. "It's me, it's me," she yelled, clutching at Djuma Misheri. This was not enough to pass as a confession.

Three of us had signed false confessions. The Libyans had what they needed to put us away for good, so they stopped torturing us. We were returned to the prison on 12 May 1999. I had been tortured almost daily for over two months. For the next fourteen months I would be isolated from the others, with only Mama Salma for company.

Mama Salma's Treasure

Salma Ali was the first person I saw at the Sharon Nasser police station. She had been assigned to superintend the women. Djuma Misheri introduced her on our first evening at the prison, with a warning that she represented him and that any bad behaviour would be reported directly to him. He treated us as though we were naughty children, telling us: "When you see Salma, see me. Whatever you have to say to me, say it to her. She will be in charge of you."

"I am your mother here and you are my children," said the woman we would come to call Mama Salma.

We had a love-hate relationship with our jailer and 'provider'. She was a contradictory character. She could in one moment be compassion itself and in another, inflict extreme cruelty. Too white for a Libyan, fat and with a face that was almost beautiful, she was probably about fifty.

After the meeting with Roumen Petrov, I was Mama Salma's exclusive prisoner. The others were kept in separate cells and had different jailers. I was a notorious captive that earned Mama Salma the respect of her colleagues and added another notch to her career belt. For almost a year I practically lived with Mama Salma—we ate together and slept in the same cell until April 2000. I shared my heartache, fear and frustration with her out of necessity.

Salma was evil. Like most primitive people, she was intoxicated by power and would wield it to the detriment of others just because she could. After my first interrogation with the electrical torture machines, I saw just how malicious Salma could be. Up until this point she had been tolerable, only laughing when she saw how badly I had been beaten. This time, however, she decided to have some fun. When I came to on the floor of my cell, I was tormented by an acute thirst because of the copious amount of drugs I had been pumped with. Salma shoved her flip-flop into the toilet and then pushed it into my mouth. "Here. Drink water!" she cackled gleefully.

Another time when I returned from the torture facility, Salma tricked me again. The electrical torture had made my muscles seize up and I couldn't move. I dropped to the floor. Salma tut-tutted like a mother hen and brought me a glass of water. Gulping down a huge sip, I realized that it was like seawater. She had salted it! "Maybe your blood pressure is down. The salt will make it better," she told me, barely stifling a giggle. When Valentina had been with me, Salma had put cayenne pepper in her water.

Once she brought me a white sheet. I was puzzled. "You know I'm not here all day long. Why don't you wrap yourself in it. The others will think it is me. Then you can go to the embassy and save yourself," she told me. I saw through her evil trick: I would probably be shot trying to escape. Maybe she was tired of looking after me, or maybe she was just bored.

"They brought me here through the front door and they will take me out through the same door. I am innocent," I stated. "If I tried to run away it would mean I am guilty."

"Wow, how smart you are," Mama Salma laughed.

I will never forgive her for these cruelties and I won't forget.

The truth is that I had opportunities to escape but I wondered whether the Bulgarian Embassy would take me in. Later I asked an embassy representative if they would have helped me. He said he did not know. I am convinced that they would have sent me back to prison. That's not what stopped me, though. An escape, even if successful, would have been a confession of guilt. If I had run away, all my suffering would have been in vain; I would have been branded a murderer.

Salma must have had some decent bones in her body, as she was capable of remorse. I took perverse pleasure in making her feel guilty about the way she treated me. I constantly criticized her about the petty cruelties she inflicted.

"It's not my fault," she would protest when I scolded her. "The *mudir* told me to," she would add.

"The *mudir* wasn't even here when you did these things," I scoffed. "The body heals, Salma, but mean words and actions under such difficult circumstances are never forgotten. You are a sadist! I will never forgive you," I told her matter-of-factly.

She would roll her eyes when I told her off. Even though she was not very bright—I would often tell her that she probably only had one brain cell—I think that she must have realized that there were truths to my comments. Slowly, the relationship changed. She started to allow me more freedom and stopped laughing at my misfortune. She trusted that I would not attempt to escape and so she left the cell door unlocked. She even let me wander the corridors occasionally. Before she had treated me like a slave; I was made to clean the corridors, wash her clothes as well as the clothes of the other prisoners—but now she just let me be. I figured that she was trying to earn my forgiveness.

Salma was a Muslim and constantly told me that Muslims were the purest people because they washed themselves five times a day before prayers. I only ever saw her give herself a cursory wash, wiping her eyes, ears, hands and feet with a wet facecloth. She told me about her children and how her son would ask, "Mother, aren't you afraid to sleep in a cell with this murderess?"

"Well, I am not afraid. There's nothing to be afraid of. We even eat from the same plate," she would tell him. The so-called plate was like a dog's bowl. We had no utensils so we ate from it using our fingers and hands. Our one meal a day was usually rice or pasta and occasionally Salma would make us tea.

Mama Salma often disappeared to tend to other business. She bought and resold just about anything, even paint. She would return to the prison in the evenings with banknotes jammed in her socks. Her biggest income stream though was the prisoners' funds. We were her cash cows. The management allocated some budget for all five of us and gave the money to her. Naturally, she kept most of it for herself.

She was like a squirrel. She hid her money in a pillow, taking it out from time to time to 'count' it. It was evident that she could not add, so I helped her. I distributed it in piles according to the banknote values, telling her: here is 700, here is 500, here is 200 and here is 130, which means you have 1,530 dinars. She could not grasp the concept and insisted that the thickest wad had the most money in it. She then piled them up against the wall and marked the overall height of the pile.

To pass the time I helped Mama Salma to calculate how much she earned for looking after me each day. She estimated it at five dinars a day. However, as she was very uneducated and she could hardly read, her calculations were always wrong. "Come on, Salma. How much is X days multiplied by X dinars?" I would prompt her. She didn't have the slightest desire to learn. She simply preferred that I did it.

While she was absent, Djuma Moloto would sometimes come to the cell. When I saw him I physically shuddered, thinking he was collecting me for further torture. "When I come here you are on tenterhooks. Relax! We're not going anywhere," he said.

Whether I wanted it or not, Salma was the most important person in my life at that time.

৵৵৵

My only trips outside the police station were to the prosecutor's office. All of us were interrogated every forty-five days and there was no torture involved. They asked me about the transfusion of poisonous substances, murdered children, the use of alcohol in public places and so forth. They read the accusations to me and I replied arrogantly in Arabic: "This is the children's hospital's problem. Why are you asking me about it? I have done nothing wrong. I want to go home." I never knew whether I would be punished for my belligerent tone.

Valentina and I were always questioned together but we travelled there independently. The authorities obviously didn't want us to have time to corroborate our stories. We were not allowed to speak to each other but we managed to swap scraps of information in the toilet. Valentina told me about Nasya's confession and about how the others had been tortured.

It was a ridiculous situation—we were called to the prosecutor's office so that there would be legal grounds to keep us in prison longer. While the state was still collecting evidence, we could be detained.

I also managed to exchange a few words with Smilyan at the prosecutor's office. Salma was very careful to keep us apart, but we found a way to talk. He told me that he had been accused of preparing the mixture containing the AIDS virus, with which I and my colleagues had allegedly injected the children.

On 31 August, God only knows why, Smilyan was released. I whispered to him through a slit in my cell wall: "Tell everybody what they have done to us. Find Emil and tell him where I am, please, that I am separated from the others." He was highly stressed, afraid that they wouldn't release him after all and only nodded as a sign that he had heard me.

His release was as unexpected and illogical as everything else that had passed before. They let him go at lunch time. He didn't know what to do, where to go or whether they would give him his documents back. They just threw him out of the police station and that was it. Smilyan walked around the jail aimlessly. Perhaps he was afraid someone would shoot him when he left or perhaps he was waiting for someone to come and pick him up. Salma shooed him away like he was a scavenging dog. By late afternoon Smilyan was still hanging around and asked Salma for something to eat. She gave him some rice. Shaking her head, she said to me: "Allah, what a fool he is! Tell him to catch a taxi and go to your embassy. Then he must hit the road to Benghazi or to Bulgaria. He is crazy to stay here."

"They must have told him to wait here for his passport," I replied. "Now you see. If he was guilty, would he really stick around here?"

At around 11pm Djuma Misheri barked, "What is he still doing here? I will have to drive him to the embassy." Ironically, the man who had arrested him ended up delivering him safely to the Bulgarian Embassy.

I didn't hear much more about him. I know that he went back to Bulgaria and I heard a rumour that he became schizophrenic.

There had been no real intervention of our behalf yet, but I remained optimistic. Then, in November 1999, we met with the first Bulgarian who was serious about getting us released. Plamen Ikonomov was the acting Bulgarian ambassador to Libya. At his office, we sat behind a desk with a chain of Libyan policemen in front of us. "No talking, no talking!" they shouted.

Ignoring our hostile guards, Plamen asked: "Did they beat you? Was there any violence?"

"No, quiet. Silence! Conversations are forbidden," a guard started yelling. "This question is not allowed. We have a doctor here who says there is nothing wrong with them!"

Plamen Ikonomov just looked at them coldly and said: "That response of yours and their silence I interpret as 'yes'. I assume that you have tortured them. Why are my fellow countrymen barefoot?" he continued.

Djuma Misheri snapped, "Well, I'm barefoot too. So what if they are barefoot?"

"I don't care about you," replied Ikonomov. "I want my fellow citizens to be shod and well. Is that how you treat our countrymen?"

Plamen informed us that our relatives had hired a very good Bulgarian lawyer for us, Vladimir Sheitanov. During the meeting, he walked all over Djuma Misheri and we finally felt that we were not alone in this nightmare. My heart almost burst with renewed hope. He then told the international media that the authorities were playing for time so they could fabricate evidence against us. He demanded immediate action and threatened to take our case further with the Bulgarian President, Prime Minister and Minister of Foreign Affairs if his demands were not met.

The Libyans complained that Plamen Ikonomov had acted totally inappropriately during the meeting with their officials and he was dismissed. Then his son died in a car crash in Libya. We feared that it had not been accidental. We never saw him again.

On 22 March 2000 we were taken to a police station where we met a lawyer, Osman Bizzanti. The Bulgarian Embassy had hired him to defend us. He wanted specifics—who had done what, what kind of torture we had endured and what our jail conditions were like. Kristiyana was very helpful because she knew all the policemen by first name and surname, while I could only describe what they looked like.

When telling him about how the dogs were turned on me, Bizzanti interjected: "Valya, do you at least know the dog's name? Then I can call it as a witness." I didn't find it very funny. That aside, he had our best interests at heart. He even visited me in jail so he could keep an eye on how Mama Salma was treating me.

I lived with Mama Salma until the spring of 2000. Finally, I was moved to the Zhdeyda prison where the others were now being kept.

Salma was out when a policeman came to collect me and for a fleeting moment I thought I would tell him where she stashed her money. I didn't though. Despite everything, I felt sorry for Salma so left her treasure intact.

Our first trial was about to begin.

Defendants

Kristiyana, Nasya, Snezhana, Valentina, Ashraf and I were transported to Diashabi, The People's Court, on 17 February 2000 to start the trial. None of us, the accused, understood what was happening and the lawyer our families had hired to defend us, Vladimir Sheitanov, was not there to represent us. Apparently, the Bulgarian state had not been informed that a trial had been scheduled and weren't even aware of the extent of the charges. I was shocked to see how my co-accused had changed—they looked haggard and old. Apart from Valentina, I had not seen the rest of them for almost a year.

Not only was our lawyer not present, there was also no interpreter or Bulgarian representative. The court was packed with angry parents of the children that had been infected with HIV. Some of them had their children with them. They kept us in what I can only describe as a cage. In the cage next to us were prisoners in striped prison garb. We thought that they might be involved in the same hearing. Their case was called first and Ashraf tried to explain what these fundamentalist Islamists were being tried for, but he couldn't hear very well over the shouting of the court spectators. The prisoners were soon handcuffed and taken away.

It was like being in a Roman arena, with everyone waiting for us to be eaten alive by lions. Mothers wept hysterically, fathers shook their fists and children wept. The judge banged his gavel for order then proceeded to read out the indictment in Arabic. Ashraf translated what he could. We had smuggled something through Turkey. What ... How ...? It was like playing broken-down-telephone. Later we studied the charge sheet and picked out a few phrases:

'Performing actions in the territory of Libya ... leading to killing of people ... assault against the security of the state—an act punishable by death. Participation in collective arrangement and conspiracy to commit a premeditated crime ... aggravating circumstances. Causing an epidemic by injecting 393 children with the AIDS virus, twenty-three of whom died by October 1999 at the children's hospital, El-Fatih, in Benghazi. An act punishable by death in the case of more than one death. Premeditated murder using substances that cause death sooner or later. Extramarital sexual relationships. Three involved in the production of alcohol; one drinking alcoholic beverages in public places; four conducting illegal foreign currency transactions.'

Although we understood only a fraction of what went on in the courtroom, we could see the whole picture for the first time and how huge the conspiracy was which we were embroiled in. They questioned Kristiyana, Nasya and Ashraf.

"You, Kristiyana, have you exchanged currency before?" the prosecutor demanded.

"Yes. I need money to live," she answered.

"Nasya, have you sent money home to your brother?"

"Yes, I have," she replied.

The hearing was a farce. The judge allowed the father of an infected child to speak his mind and a man subsequently slipped into the cage and beat Ashraf. It was a relief to be taken back to prison. However, before we left our car was surrounded by furious Libyans, shouting and banging against the door.

"Get down! Get down on the floor!" Djuma Moloto shouted at me.

"I haven't done anything wrong. Why should I hide? I'm tired of you," I shouted back.

"They will kill us both. You have killed so many children!" he exclaimed.

"So what if they kill you?" I answered. "We are not to blame for this.

You Libyan policeman have allowed the real culprits to get away with it," I said. He took off at speed and the people dispersed.

The second hearing was on 28 February and thankfully we had our lawyer representing us. We were sitting in our cage and waiting for the travesty to start when Nasya said, "Valya, Emil is in the courtroom. He's sitting there on the benches." I didn't react. I was afraid to look at him because my interrogators had often threatened to kill my family. I pretended I didn't know him. I thought that they might target Emil to get me to confess to their accusations.

We had been apart for a little over a year. I had last seen him on 9 February 1999. I longed to hear his voice, to look at him and to hug him. It pained me terribly not to be able to even make eye contact in that courtroom.

At the same hearing, Nasya, Ashraf and Kristiyana recanted the testimonies they had given. "All the things I said during the police interrogation were extorted through excruciating torture," Kristiyana said. "The police electrocuted and beat me. It was worse than being in a medieval torture chamber," she added.

The hearing was then adjourned.

Emil had attempted to see me several times in prison but had been turned away. He was finally allowed to visit me at The People's Court. His support meant everything to me. Apparently he was not in danger. Some might think that my fear for his safety was irrational, but after all I had been through, I believed the Libyans capable of killing him to make me cooperate.

We had no privacy. In front of cameras and reporters I told him everything that had happened, sparing him none of the details. I summed up all the horrors I had been through in a few minutes. Listening to my story, he became deathly pale. He said he was going to faint and began laughing hysterically.

The next visits were at the police station and we were watched over by guards. Emil tried to lift my spirits. He brought pictures and letters from the children, which I wasn't allowed to read. He told me that Fatma's family were praying for me, constantly asking whether there was any news about how I was doing. They believed in my innocence and it touched me deeply. They had also supported Emil when so many had turned their backs on him, not wanting to be associated with either of us.

He wrote down the names of the torturers I could remember and gave them to our attorney. The Libyans must have wised up to the fact that he was helping me and forbade him from visiting. A huge, frightening black man interrupted one of our visits, shouting, "What is the husband of that Bulgarian doing here? Take him away right now! Who let him in here?"

Two days later, shortly before my birthday, Emil brought me a cake and bad news. "We will not be able to see each other here anymore. They won't let me come back," he said.

The next day I was visited by our Libyan-appointed lawyer, Osman Bizzanti. He asked me how they were treating me and whether they were beating me.

"I'm alright. Everything's okay. They aren't beating me," I said. "I want to see my husband but they won't let me."

"Your husband? Yesterday your husband was sent to Bulgaria by your embassy," he informed me.

"I do not understand. I want to see my husband," I insisted.

"Okay, okay. I'll try to arrange that."

Emil had left the country. Lyudmil Spassov, the Bulgarian ambassador, was afraid that Emil would discuss details about the case with the press and paint the Bulgarian Embassy in a bad light. So he made sure that he went back to Bulgaria. Emil, though, made a point of enlightening the Bulgarian media to the real facts surrounding our detention and torture.

Bulgarian newspapers had learned that a group of nurses were being questioned by Libyan police four days after we were taken to Tripoli. However, they took the Libyans' statement at face value when they implied that we were simply being interviewed as witnesses. The Bulgarian Embassy, on the other hand, was aware that we had been accused of infecting the children with HIV, but they kept things quiet, believing that diplomatic intervention could possibly make things worse for us. Their passivity enabled the Libyans to get away with barbaric torture.

Our story had been forgotten. Until the trial started. Kristiyana's description of the torture we had suffered made headlines.

❧ ❧ ❧

A media furore ensued. The Bulgarian press took up our story with vigour. The TV show 'Exiles' even called for a candle-lit vigil in front of the Libyan Embassy to show their support. The Libyan Ambassador in Bulgaria was quick to react to the overnight media attention, stating: "Such events do not contribute to the development of our bilateral relations. We urge the Bulgarian Government not to allow such events in the future."

To our immense disappointment, Ivan Kostov, then Prime Minister of Bulgaria said in an interview: "Well, what if they are guilty ... ?" The most influential person in Bulgaria did not defend our innocence. The Libyan Embassy capitalized on this, stating: "We highly appreciate the reasonable and committed position contained in the statements of Prime Minister Kostov."

One day we were visited by the chief prosecutor of Bulgaria, Nikola

Filchev. He had come to argue on our behalf that we should be defended by a Bulgarian lawyer. A man called Emil Manolov had us sign documents authorizing Vladimir Sheitanov to represent us. We put pen to paper without knowing anything about our lawyer's credentials. I did ask Manolov about him but a Libyan policeman shouted, "No talking!" and that was that.

Later that day we were taken to the office of the General of the Libyan Judicial Police at The People's Court. We had no idea what was happening. For the first time we were officially allowed to talk to each other. We were even offered cigarettes. Nikola Filchev and a few Bulgarians were also in the office. Filchev told us that he was not allowed to discuss the trial with us, adding, "I hope you're not involved."

Emil Manolov introduced himself again.

"We met this morning," he said.

"But who you are?" we asked.

"I am the consul from Bulgaria. I'm working on your case," he told us.

The atmosphere was oppressive: The Libyans wouldn't let us ask questions and our compatriots couldn't tell us much. Each nation had an interpreter. The Bulgarian interpreter was a man called Boreto. The Libyans' interpreter was an old lady. To our surprise, we learned that she was Bulgarian. She kept interrupting Boreto, insisting that he explain every single word we said to the Libyans.

"Why don't you translate what the Bulgarians are saying," Boreto asked.

"I can't translate for them," she snapped. "I'm on the other side. I'm here with the Libyans," she added.

We were shocked. A Bulgarian woman, a total stranger, was siding with the Libyans. She didn't care about us in the least. We later found out that her daughter, Tony, was also a nurse and the General's mistress. The Bulgarian woman had come to Libya to help look after her daughter's child. Since the meeting was in the General's office, the older woman was asked to act as an interpreter for the Libyans. It never occurred to her that we might be innocent. After the meeting I thought about this woman incessantly. I am sure that she told the Libyans that we were guilty, even if just to deflect attention away from her daughter. That woman made me very bitter.

All these examples of Bulgarian carelessness, indifference and doubt mentally crushed us. For months we had been tortured by the Libyans so that we would confess to monstrous crimes. Three of us had crumbled. Despite having been forcibly removed from our loved ones and inhumanely tortured, what destroyed us was the lack of support from fellow Bulgarians.

All we could hope for was a fair trial.

Case No. 44/99

According to the Bulgarian Telegraph Agency, a citizen claiming to be a relative of the Palestinian man (Ashraf) accused in Case 44/99, stated to the Bulgarian Embassy in Washington in March 2000: "All the Bulgarians and the Palestinian have been tortured with electrical current and in other ways, which can be proven by an independent judicial expert. This was done to conceal the real culprits, who are associated with the Libyan supreme authorities."

Five days later, the Bulgarian Ambassador, Lyudmil Spassov, met with the Libyan Foreign Minister, Abdel Rahman Shalgam, and told him that "the Bulgarian State believes in the innocence of the Bulgarian citizens, but the court is the one who should decide this, based solely on facts and evidence".

Shalgam stated that the Bulgarian newspapers used a tone that denoted racism and levelled unbridled attacks and accusations at the Libyan authorities. He urged the Bulgarian authorities to disassociate themselves from those statements made by the press.

At the same time, Paris-based Professor Montagnier from the Louis Pasteur Institute—a renowned virologist co-accredited with Professor Vittorio Colizzi for discovering AIDS—provided testimony on the HIV infection in Libya, suggesting that the infection in Benghazi was hospital-induced and most likely caused by the re-use of syringes or when collecting blood. According to him, the probability of infection by vaccination was small as some of the HIV-infected children were already 15 years old.

Many influential people and institutions started to actively support us. The State Secretary of the Vatican received an official letter describing our case after the Bulgarian Foreign Minister, Nadezhda Mihailova, sought contact with Pope John Paul II and several countries publicly demanded that we be granted a fair trial.

We, of course, had no information about all this while it was happening.

On 17 April 2000 we were moved to the so-called 'exemplary' cells. I was in a metre-and-a-half by a metre-and-a-half cell with Valentina. When we were moved I was scared, crying hysterically and telling the others: "That's it! There is no escape from here." Valentina calmed me down, saying, "Don't worry. We'll manage somehow!" I couldn't see how we would manage in this dungeon. We would surely go insane in such a tiny space. Valentina was short and even she couldn't lie down diagonally in the cell. We adopted impossible positions to coexist in a space where every centimetre was precious. How the other three, Nasya, Snezhana and Kristiyana, fitted in their cell, I can only imagine. Their cell was somewhat longer, so they could stretch out when lying down, like sardines in a tin.

The very first day, when the guards brought us 'food', other prisoners gathered to see us, the murderers. I was shocked to see that there were also two or three children among them. That was my next lesson in Arab justice: mothers punished for having illegitimate or extramarital children are imprisoned with their children or else give birth to their children in prison. The children are then raised in jail and sometimes die because of the conditions ...

A one- or two-year-old child ran to our cell and hugged me. I broke down in tears when he pressed his little body to me. I embraced and petted him, asking, "Why are you here? What is your name?"

His name was Kadri. It felt so good to hold him. An inmate started shouting, "One of the killers has got Kadri!" His mother hurried over, saw how we were cuddled and said, "What are you shouting about? What kind of killers are these? Children are never wrong—these women can't be killers." I was grateful to her. In prison I at last met someone who believed we were innocent. This woman had been imprisoned because Kadri was an illegitimate child.

Shortly before I was moved, Emil smuggled me some food from outside—chocolate and eggs—which I shared with the others. On the fifth day we ran out of our supplies. The guards gave us only salted water, sometimes with something extra in it—red worms. We had a few lemons and a sachet of sugar, so Nasya removed the worms, put some lemon juice and sugar in the water to kill the salty taste and we drank the result. We were always thirsty.

Suffocating in our narrow cells, we insisted on seeing our Libyan lawyer, Osman Bizzanti. For nine days we had survived with barely any air or space and for four days on only worm-infested water. Our only connection with the outside world was a small piece of sky visible from the corridor in front of the cells. It was the only thing reminding us that there was life outside of prison. It was a creepy and scary thought.

Finally he came and managed to get us moved into a large common cell with a window that wasn't blacked out. We even had access to the yard where we could stretch our legs. In the cell, we became friends with some of the Libyan inmates, especially Kadri's mother. We would often play with Kadri and looked after him until mother and son were eventually released. We also got to know some of the other women and I made many friends in Zhdeyda. They supported us and their children uplifted our spirits and made us feel alive. We five Bulgarian women, roommates by necessity, also grew closer and shared stories of our lives from before this nightmare as well as what we had endured when being tortured. Initially we had only one blanket and slept on the floor. Then we were tossed two mattresses, one of which I shared with Valentina. The embassy intervened and ensured we each received our own mattress.

One day we were taken to The People's Court to meet with the envoy of the then Bulgarian President Stoyanov. We met with a lawyer called Hristo Danov. He obtained the right for us to be taken out of prison once a month to meet with our diplomats. Later on we persuaded the people at the embassy to bring us basic necessities at the prison each week.

One day, the executive director of Muammar al-Gaddafi's son's foundation, the Gaddafi International Foundation for Charity Associations (GICDF) arrived at the prison, inviting us to the director's office of the women's wing for a meeting. We were in our pyjamas, dishevelled and unprepared. We hastily put on some clothes and hurried to meet the director. A Libyan man along with Ambassador Lyudmil Spassov and Roumen Petrov waited for us outside the office. The ambassador told us, "This is a very important person. He will help you; he is on your side." Saleh Abdel Salam, executive director of GICDF, was intimidating. We didn't realize it then, but this Libyan man would indeed help us in the future.

The trial progressed slowly, with one continuance after another. Our first ray of hope arrived via an official letter to the court by Professor Luc Perrin, an AIDS specialist. In it he strongly expressed that "the outbreak at the Benghazi hospital was caused by three blood-transferred viruses: AIDS (N1U), hepatitis C (NSU) and hepatitis B (NMU) and is due solely to a hospital-induced (nosocomial) infection. The spread of these viruses is due to improper medical manipulations with improperly sterilized and repeatedly used instruments and needles". He cited several examples to support his assertion, including the Vienna hospital HIV outbreak in September 1999 ascribed to poor sanitation and sexual transmission of the infection by infected fathers. The next month Bizzanti enlisted Perrin as a consultant.

The intervention of a leading professional such as Perrin gave us much hope, which we kept alive in the letters we were finally allowed to send to our relatives at Christmas. Unbeknown to us, the Libyans were reading our letters. I had written in one that 'the Arabs with their animal instincts know how to manipulate and frighten us ...' A guard came to me, shouting, "You think we are animals here?" Subsequently, we were all forbidden to write to our relatives. Fortunately, Emil Manolov got this ruling reversed. However, we were made to understand that the Libyans would not send any letters that were unflattering to them.

In April 2001 we heard that Gaddafi had remarked that the CIA had successfully created HIV in its laboratories and that the Benghazi epidemic was a massive experiment conducted by us with the backing of the CIA or Mossad. We worried that our indictment might have been pay-back for the Lockerbie bombing, in which a Libyan man had been found guilty of planting a bomb on Pan Am Flight 103, with the Libyans all the while crying foul that it was a set-up. Such statements demonstrated that this trial had huge political implications and that Muammar al-Gaddafi would ultimately decide our fate.

Despite Bizzanti's efforts, we believed that everything was stacked against us, that we were merely unwilling participants in a ridiculous play where it didn't matter what we said or did or how good our lawyer was. After all they had put us through, there was no way they would release us to tell the real story.

In court I listened to a Libyan woman testifying against me. She said I chased her from a room and injected a child, which she accidentally saw. He apparently vomited right afterwards. I was sure I had never seen this woman before and had certainly not attended to her at the hospital. She was no doubt paid to lie under oath.

Nasya was identified by a father of twins as an accomplice. This man looked like he was a drug addict who had been dragged off the streets to testify. Nasya's 'crime' was allegedly committed in the reception room where she worked. However, Nasya Kisimova worked in reception, not Nasya Nenova. The bastards hadn't even realized that this was a completely different person! The man pointed out Nasya Nenova, even though Nasya Kisimova looked completely different—one was blond and the other dark-haired. Nasya Nenova never worked in reception but the court accepted his testimony ...

A policeman testified against Kristiyana. The prosecution showed a video of the police breaking into Kristiyana's home, allegedly for the first time. They made a cursory search then looked in some cupboards and voilà! Bags of blood. Kristiyana admitted on the stand that she kept empty blood bags at home, but in the bathroom. They had evidently moved them. Abdul Madjit Schol, known as 'The Chemist', was present during the raid and told the policemen: "Do not touch this. There's AIDS virus in it!" How he knew this just by looking is laughable. When the witness was questioned on this point he grew very uneasy. It was obvious he had learned his words but could not diverge from the testimony he had rehearsed. He collapsed at the end of his testimony.

No Bulgarians testified against us. However, I suspect many of the original seventeen nurses who had been arrested fingered us so that they would be released. I am certain that Maria did. Back home, when Bulgaria Nova TV interviewed her, she didn't divulge what she had been asked in her interrogations. She said she didn't remember anything about it. I know for a fact that the policemen set dogs on Maria and she literally shat in her pants. How can you forget something like this? She said nothing because she felt guilty or maybe she was still scared that the Libyans would come after her.

In May 2001 we were allowed to see our relatives. Nasya's husband Ivan and my daughter Tony obtained visas along with some journalists from the Bulgarian electronic media and the newspaper *Monitor*. Bulgarian journalists from major newspapers who wrote harshly about the Libyans were not admitted. I had no idea that my daughter was in Libya. It was yet another day in court and we were each being questioned about the alleged torture, although only a question or two were permitted. I had my head down while one of the others was being questioned and was thinking of how I had got involved in this horror. Suddenly, I heard the unmistakable voice of my daughter crying out: "Mommy, Mommy!" I had not seen Tony for three years. My heart felt like it would burst. "Mom, keep your chin up! You are innocent; the whole world supports you and knows you are innocent," Tony shouted. This would sustain me in the long hours in prison and in my most difficult moments I would replay her voice.

She was with Ashraf's sisters, who also began to shout that we were innocent. They were all promptly expelled from court. I worried when I did not see her face in the courtroom when the trial resumed the following afternoon. I prayed that she was unharmed. Thankfully I saw her in court a few days later.

During her month-long stay in Libya we managed to meet four times—twice at the hearing and twice at the prison. When we first saw each other, we didn't know what to say. I cannot describe how I felt when she was so close to me, when I heard her voice and stroked her hair ... She had grown up, changed and was committed to lifting my spirit. I tried to hold my emotions in check in front of her because I didn't want to upset her further but after she left I broke down. I missed everyone so much.

On the same day that Tony and Ashraf's sisters had caused a scene at The People's Court, a television station broadcast Nasya's tearful reunion with her husband. The world watched their emotional exchange:

"How is our child?" Nasya asked.

"Everything is okay. Don't worry," he reassured her.

"Are mom and dad well?"

"Everybody is well and says hello. We love you very much!" he said.

"I love you very much too. I miss you all very much!" Nasya sobbed.

"Do you need anything?" he asked.

"I want to come home ..."

"You will! You will come home, don't worry."

In July the Bulgarian elections were won by a newly established party headed by the former king of Bulgaria, Simeon Saxe-Coburg. Solomon Passy was given the position of Foreign Minister. At his first press conference he said that our case was a major priority for the Bulgarian Ministry of Foreign Affairs and we met the new President of Parliament and some representatives of the Foreign Ministry shortly thereafter. We were also moved into new cells.

On 22 September 2001 the court was supposed to pass judgment on the case. It was postponed for three months. Solomon Passy told the media in Bulgaria this was good news. "We have some indication of preparations for a clear and transparent trial and hope that on the 22nd of December we will be able to achieve what we all dream about," he said.

We first met Passy in person in October. We had been instructed that we should dress formally for the meeting with the Foreign Minister but had nothing to wear. We begged the other prisoners to lend us some of their better clothes. I borrowed a pair of trousers from one inmate and a jacket from another, a shirt from a third—but I could not for the life of me find any suitable shoes. In desperation, I borrowed a pair of sabots, a type of clog, and covered them as best I could with the trousers. I had to trade my sneakers for them.

We were finally going to meet an important statesman and we were very tense.

However, he was exceptionally friendly and we immediately trusted him. He always supported us, publicly and in private. He also ensured

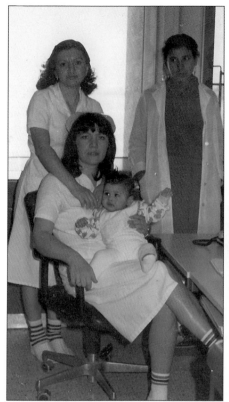

Left: During my first stay in Libya working conditions in the hospital at Tarhuna were on par with European standards. (*photo* Deian Yotov, *Trud* newspaper)

Below: In the 1980s it never crossed my mind that my job as a nurse would cost me eight years of my life. (*photo* Valya Chervenyashka's collection)

Bottom: Tarhuna hospital. (*photo* Valya Chervenyashka's collection)

Top left: The November 1998 cover of *LA* magazine. *LA* was the first to publish revelations about the AIDS epidemic at the Benghazi Children Hospital. I didn't imagine that together with four other Bulgarian nurses I looked like this to so many Libyans. (*photo LA* magazine / internet)

Top right: Djuma Misheri, nicknamed 'The Dog', in typical pose, 2007. He directed the regime of torture against us. (*photo* Deian Yotov, *Trud* newspaper)

Above left: Stills from the police movie in which police officers, led by Djuma Misheri, are breaking into Kristiyana's apartment. (*photo* Bulgarian Telegraph Agency)

Above right: Misheri's face makes me bristle with anger; the man who dragged me through hell. This face refuses to get out of my mind and haunts me still. (*photo* Bulgarian Telegraph Agency)

Top left: This is one of the first images of our case, taken by a Bulgarian journalist. Valentina, I and Kristiyana are alongside our eternal companions: the bars. (*photo* Georgi Milkov, *24 Hours* newspaper)

Top right: That's us, the five defendants. At that time I imagined that all would come to pass and awaited my death every single moment of every single day. (*photo* Georgi Milkov, *24 Hours* newspaper)

Above: Our first meeting with the Bulgarian Foreign Minister, Solomon Passy and the pavilion where he welcomed us. He took our case to heart. (*photo* Bulgarian Telegraph Agency)

Right: This is what it looked like outside the court during the hearings. They protected us, the vile murderers, from the parents of the infected children. (*photo* BGNES News Agency)

Below: Snezhana, me, Kristiyana and Zdravko in anticipation of what will come next in our personal nightmares. (*photo* Valya Chervenyashka's collection)

A meeting with representatives of the Bulgarian Government. (*photo* Valya Chervenyashka's collection)

Me and Nasya: side by side by necessity, looking in different directions. (*photo* Bulgarian Telegraph Agency)

Above: While we were paying for the sins of the Libyan State against its own children, the parents were organizing meetings, demanding our deaths. (*photo* BGNES News Agency)

Left: Me and Mabruka in her cell. (*photo* Valya Chervenyashka's collection)

Below: Mabruka and I tried to make our lives as close to normal as possible. (*photo* Valya Chervenyashka's collection)

Top left: Me, Zdravko and Kristiyana enjoying the company of several tortoises brought to The House by the policemen who guarded us. Gradually we got used to the presence of our guards who treated us as innocents. (*photo* Valya Chervenyashka's collection)

Above: In moments like this I almost felt like a complete person. (*photo* Valya Chervenyashka's collection)

Top right: With my husband Emil during his visit to The House. (*photo* Valya Chervenyashka's collection)

Right: With one of my daughters at The House. (*photo* Valya Chervenyashka's collection)

With one of
Ashraf's sisters
during her visit
to The House.
(*photo* Valya
Chervenyashka's
collection)

A policemen
perjures
himself on his
involvement
with the squad
that allegedly
found bags of
blood containing
the HIV virus
in Kristiyana's
apartment. (*photo*
Deian Yotov, *Trud*
newspaper)

With one of my daughters
visiting me in prison. (*photo*
Valya Chervenyashka's
collection)

Years were passing and the uncertainty ate away at us. Kristiyana, me and Valentina behind the bars that separated us from the world, seemingly forever. (*photo* Georgi Milkov, *24 Hours* newspaper)

No matter how many judicial arguments and cases I heard, I always knew we were mere puppets in the Libyan scheme of things. (*photo* Georgi Milkov, *24 Hours* newspaper)

Another day in court, May 2006. (*photo* Deian Yotov, *Trud* newspaper)

Above: While we contemplated our fate the parents of the infected children were outside the court, crying for the lost lives of their children, May 2006. (*photo* Deian Yotov, *Trud* newspaper)

Left: 20 May, 2006; we were desperate. (*photo* Deian Yotov, *Trud* newspaper)

Below: In court listening to the testimony against us, 29 August, 2006. (*photo* Deian Yotov, *Trud* newspaper)

Left: Meeting our defence lawyers in front of the cameras, 22 April, 2006. (*photo* Deian Yotov, *Trud* newspaper)

Below: Bulgarian health workers in a metal cage in a Benghazi court, Libya, in this 2003 file photo. On Thursday, 6 May, 2004 a Libyan court condemned the nurses, accused of deliberately infecting children with HIV, to death by firing squad. (*photo* Associated Press, *text* Bulgarian Telegraph Agency)

Right: While we waited for the next death sentence, Bulgarians protested in front of the Libyan embassy, 18 December, 2006 (*photo* BGNES News Agency)

Below: With our Libyan attorney, Osman Bizzanti. (*photo* Georgi Milkov, *24 Hours* newspaper)

Me, Valentina and Kristiyana, waiting for death. (*photo* Deian Yotov, *Trud* newspaper)

Djuma Misheri during his trial accused of our torture. As usual, he doesn't look worried, knowing full well that no matter what he has done, he'll get away with it. (*photo* Deian Yotov, *Trud* newspaper)

Our tormentors' attorneys during their trial. (*photo* Deian Yotov, *Trud* newspaper)

A cold, formal meeting with the President of Bulgaria, Georgi Parvanov. (*photo* BGNES News Agency)

Relatives of the infected children carrying their portraits. Some of the children pictured here are now dead. While the real culprits were safely out of sight, the bitter anguish of the children's relatives was directed at us. (*photo* BGNES News Agency)

28 March, 2007, Sofia. During the European Championship Group G qualification football match the entire crowd demonstrated that we were not alone. (*photo* Bulgarian Telegraph Agency)

Above: On 12 May, 2007 tens of thousands of people gathered in Sofia to pray for our salvation. At the same time thousand of Bulgarians abroad queued at embassies to get ribbons of support. (*photo* BGNES News Agency)

Left: George Michael during his Sofia concert wearing a 'You Are Not Alone' ribbon. Bianca Jagger was also among the celebrities who supported the campaign. (*photo* Nikolay Yordanov's collection)

Left: On the French presidential plane minutes after leaving Libya, with Cecilia Sarcozy and Benita Ferrero-Waldner. (*photo* Cecilia Attias Foundation for Women / http://www.ceciliaattiasfoundation.org/)

Above: I embrace Kristiyana's son. (*photo* BGNES News Agency)

Right: That's me today. This is a still taken during the 'Clairvoyants' show. During shooting, the idea of writing this book was born. (*photo* Ivelina Dimitrova, Global Films)

that we met privately so we could talk freely and made sure we received things that we were lacking.

Christmas passed and so did New Year's Eve. February heralded the third anniversary of our kidnapping in Benghazi. On 17 February 2002 we prepared ourselves for the 'final' judgement. We wanted some kind of resolution to this nightmare and eagerly awaited the verdict, hoping for the best but prepared for the worst—death sentences. The People's Court didn't reach a verdict. The judge decided that there was no evidence to support the defence's charge of conspiracy against the Libyan state, maintaining that it had "fabricated an interpretation that comprised conclusions taken out of context".

The case was transferred to the Attorney General's office because the judge felt that it fell outside his court's jurisdiction. He did stress that there was no conclusive evidence of the defendants' criminal intent in offences against state security. So, allegations of conspiracy were dropped but all other charges would be heard and addressed by a different court.

My Sins against Nasya

Time in jail passed slowly between hearings. When various courses at the prison were instituted—sewing, embroidery, drawing and Arabic—we were ecstatic. They provided a relief from the monotony of prison life and allowed us to escape our cell for two hours each day. I spoke a smattering of Arabic, learned through my work at the hospital and working for Fatma's family. I started the Arabic course, thinking it might help me understand more of what was going on in the trial. Kristiyana and Nasya opted for the embroidery course.

We creatively filled the endless hours by designing our own crosswords, using paper and pencils borrowed from a guard. Then we made a backgammon board from a piece of cardboard found in the yard. We used five coins to represent the pieces, marking them with either blue or red pen. Fashioning dice was more difficult. Another inmate donated a branch but we still needed a knife to cut it. A guard eventually complied with Valentina's persistent requests for one. The next challenge was to make dots on the dice, which we accomplished using a sharp-ended stick. To my knowledge, Valentina still keeps these in her handbag to remind her of all we went through.

While the guards were aware of our contraband, they had bigger issues to contend with—gambling and drugs. The Nigerians were the drug kingpins. Sometimes Valentina and I smoked the odd cigarette with Nigerian inmates, who would say, "Sisters, we smoke other cigarettes. Do you want?"

Hashish was not an option. The thought of getting into more trouble was a pretty persuasive deterrent. We had been accused of all sorts of lesser crimes in addition to allegedly infecting the children with HIV at the children's hospital—brewing alcohol illegally, having extramarital relations and God knew what else—but dealing or using drugs had been left off our charge sheet. We didn't want to give the Libyans a valid excuse to accuse us of yet another crime. We were sure that the 'minor' offenses were included so the authorities could 'legitimately' keep us in prison while they fabricated evidence and because they wanted to convince the Libyan public that we were monsters. Besides, the cells were routinely searched for drugs by dogs.

We asked our embassy to provide us with a pack of cards. We usually played bridge. Nasya was not a good loser and I would taunt her by shouting out, "Wow, with these cards, I am not lucky," even when I had a good hand. Nasya would glare at me with hatred in her eyes. Which is no surprise—we didn't get on.

One day Kristiyana was taken away without any explanation. She was gone for five or six hours. We were incredibly worried that she was being tortured. We managed to get word to the embassy. When she returned to the cell, she was highly agitated and we gave her some contraband Lexotan to calm her down. She told us she had been questioned somewhere in Tripoli by people from GICDF and a top secret service agent. We prayed that the embassy would send someone to meet with us but we had no idea when and if this would occur. We bribed a Libyan guard in the yard to let us know if they came.

The consul Sergey Yankov and the interpreter Boreto arrived the next morning. We were grateful, especially as they left us three bags of goods in the luggage room. Later, on opening them, we complained among ourselves that Libyan inmates received much more than we did. It may seem petty that we felt aggrieved, but we did.

When we met with them we demanded answers. What was happening? Why were we being interrogated again? Should we agree to go with them? Should we answer their questions or refuse? What should we do? Suddenly a fight broke out in the luggage room.

Yankov and Boreto were frightened and beat a hasty retreat.

"We don't know what you should do," they said. "We have to go. We don't want to be beaten up."

"Tell us what to do," we pleaded.

"We're scared they might take us one by one and kill us," I said.

"Do whatever you feel is right," they said, then left.

It was unbelievable that our countrymen abandoned us like that but, at the same time, it strengthened our solidarity. It was us against the world, we thought.

One Friday we had a really nice jailer. She let us stay outside longer than the usual hour allocated to inmates. She even let Valentina and I use the kitchen. In our bag of goodies from the embassy we had rice, onions, peppers, milk powder, sugar and spices. Valentina combined the rice, onion and spices to make a stuffing for the peppers then started on a sauce. She put the casserole dish on the floor as there was no table. Bending down to pick something up off the floor, I accidentally knocked the sugar into the saucepan. "Valya, look what you have done," Valentina scolded. The sauce was ruined. Thankfully we still had the stuffed peppers to eat. What a feast it was. We didn't know when we would get this lucky again.

The other prisoners saw us as interchangeable, calling us "the Bulgarian medics". However, we were very different people. I was closest to Valentina, probably because we spent the most time together. We just clicked. She was a wonderful, quirky person. She was creative and liked to make things, which she did very slowly, so I called her 'Slowgine'. Soon everybody started calling her that. Initially she was angry with me for giving her this nickname, as she felt it was insulting, but she soon realized that we all meant it affectionately. I also got along very well with Kristiyana, who was very easy-going. Snezhana mostly kept to herself so I didn't get to know her well. From what I saw, she was a little self-absorbed and was certainly not the first to put her hand up when help was needed. Nasya was also introverted but she had a good heart. I never thought of her as a friend though.

When we had birthdays, although we really didn't feel like celebrating, the others would club in to buy a small present from the prison shop— usually a bar of soap or some such thing. However, our group was not altogether harmonious and after a visit from Bizzanti one day, tensions escalated. He lost his temper, shouting at Nasya, Ashraf and Kristiyana, "How could you? How could you say you infected the children?" In the next breath, he praised me for not giving in. "Valya, you are a strong woman for not confessing. If the others were like you, this would be much easier."

An invisible wall went up between those who had confessed and those who hadn't.

Every time we were scheduled to go to court, we would get short-tempered with each other. I felt intense anger toward Nasya and her every mannerism irritated me. Once, when I was making a tomato sauce on a hot plate we had smuggled into our cell, Nasya accidentally dropped her soap into the sauce. I was livid. If a hearing had not been imminent I probably would have laughed about it. Another time I was so annoyed with her—I can't remember what for—that I raised my hand to slap her. She cringed like a dog. I lowered my hand, ashamed. She looked so vulnerable.

I couldn't forgive her for the false confession she had made because she had never said she was sorry—not once. As such, I did not respect Nasya. I thought she was a coward. Kristiyana and Ashraf, on the other hand, recanted in court and apologized profusely to Snezhana and me. I reassured them that I did not bear a grudge and that I understood why they had done it—Ashraf feared for the safety of his parents and sisters and Kristiyana just could not withstand any more pain.

Ultimately, the majority of the indictment was based on Nasya's testimony.

Eventually my rage boiled over and I had it out with Nasya. On the way to a hearing I said to her, "In the car tomorrow, you will sit on the other side. Far away from me. When they give us the death penalty, it will be because of you."

I wasn't the only one to lose my temper before hearings. We would all quarrel over the smallest things, like a cup that had been moved, and pick fights with one another. Our anger stemmed from the terror we felt. We didn't know what would become of us.

One day another inmate, a Libyan called Mabruka called me into her cell and berated me for the way I was treating Nasya. "Valya, Allah doesn't kill and he doesn't begrudge people. You know that Nasya is as innocent as you are. You don't need to keep making her feel bad. You only hurt yourself," she said. "We Libyans are good psychologists, yes?"

These wise words came from a woman who would become a true friend. She made me realize that Nasya was ridden with remorse, even if she didn't show it. I felt ashamed and stopped being cruel to her. She was in the same boat as us and gradually I forgave her.

Mabruka

Every morning we were let out for five minutes to throw away our garbage. We would either go into the yard or kitchen. During this time we could walk about freely and the guards paid us little attention. Once Valentina and I stole coffee from the kitchen then proceeded to the section of the prison where the drug dealers were housed. Most of them were Nigerian. We squatted on the floor with them, drinking our coffee and smoking cigarettes. A prisoner told the guards that we were in their cell and a policewoman promptly arrived. "What are you doing here?" she shouted.

Our misdemeanour was reported to the director, who called us to her office. She questioned us one at a time. I was first up.

"What were you doing there?" she demanded.

"I was smoking."

"Who gave you permission to go in there?" she asked.

"The door was open so we went in," I replied.

"Who did you go with?"

"With Valentina. What's the big deal? I'm still in jail," I said belligerently.

My rudeness resulted in solitary confinement. I was handcuffed and taken away. Valentina was fortunate in that she only got a verbal reprimand.

My big mouth would often get me into trouble and sent to the lock-up room. I resented being treated like a child, being told what I could and could not do. I was not a criminal and I did not want to be treated like one. I was hostile toward the prison guards and I paid for this. My wrists often bore bruises from being handcuffed.

When we first started sharing a cell with other inmates, the women were derogatory and labelled us as 'baby killers', but after a while most of them came to believe in our innocence.

"Ha! The fathers of these children have been with Moroccan girls," one said. "That is where the AIDS comes from!"

"Libyan men would never admit such a thing," another added. "That's why they caught you—because you're weak and because you are women."

The fact that they believed in our innocence was extremely important to me. They even called us 'sisters'. "Sisters, you are innocent," they reassured us. "You will get out of here; you will go home. Those people in Benghazi are dirty. They probably deserve this." Although I didn't condone that any of the children deserved to be infected with HIV, I appreciated their support.

Salma would often pop into our cell, saying, "Mother is here." We turned our backs on her and sometimes we told her to leave us alone. The prison authorities took heed that we didn't want Salma to supervise us and she was not transferred from Sharon Nasser. She was hurt and couldn't understand why we were acting so coldly toward her. I don't think she comprehended just how cruel she had been at the other prison.

Our cell had a big window overlooking the yard, starting about two metres up. It had a wide ledge that we could sit on. I put Valentina on my shoulders so she could climb up, then the others hoisted me up. Nasya came up only once. She was afraid of heights, so the others quickly helped her down. Valentina and I, however, constantly hung out the windows like monkeys, shouting at the prisoners in the yard: "Give us a cigarette, *hobi*." (*Hobi* means 'love' in Arabic.)

I first spotted Mabruka from my perch. She was a privileged prisoner in that she got to make coffee for a Libyan general in his office at the prison. He saw to it that she was moved from our cell into a much bigger cell. She was also allowed to have a TV. When she walked past our window I asked her for a cigarette.

"I don't smoke, but I will find one for you," she replied. "How many do you want?"

"Two please."

She brought one for me and one for Valentina.

"Are you Bulgarian? What is your name?"

"I am Bulgarian. I am called Valya. And you?"

"Mabruka."

This was the beginning of a strong friendship. She often said that she liked me from the very first moment when I had asked her for a cigarette and that she immediately saw that we would click.

When I met Mabruka she was about thirty-five years old. She was very pretty and was tall. She had been sentenced to fifteen years because she had stabbed a man in the heart and killed him. Her story was tragic, as were most prisoners'. Her husband had died in a car crash. Because she was beautiful, she soon attracted unwanted attention from an admirer. Though she made it clear that she was not interested in a relationship with him, he would not take no for an answer and badgered her constantly. He started stalking her. She complained to the police several times, but nobody did anything about it. Then one day she went to hospital for a check-up and found that he had followed her there. She was afraid of him. She told him to go away and he became aggressive, calling her a whore in front of the staff and patients. Mabruka had started carrying a knife because she was worried that his obsessive pursuit of her might lead to violence. She withdrew it from her bag and stabbed him. He died on the spot.

In the eyes of society, Mabruka was a criminal. However, even the courts recognized that she had been driven to kill the man who hounded her night and day. She was a devout Muslim but was broad-minded about others' beliefs. Her obvious good character and values ultimately saved her from receiving a death sentence. In Libya the penalty for murder is death unless there are valid extenuating circumstances. For instance, I learned of a Nigerian woman who killed her husband by hitting him on the back. Even though she didn't intend to kill him, she received a death sentence. The fact that Mabruka didn't spoke volumes.

We talked every day. In the mornings and evenings we would chat while she was in the yard. Then, when we were allowed our hour outside, I made it a habit of going to her cell, where we would sometimes watch television together. Valentina often came with me. Mabruka would make us tea or coffee and gave us sandwiches or eggs to eat, a welcome change from the usual rice or noodles. She was in charge of the food stores so she had access to a range of foodstuffs. Mabruka also arranged for us to get the hot plate for our cell. We gave her five dinars, which she gave to a policewoman to buy it for us. Being able to cook gave us great joy. One really appreciates the little things like this in prison.

I also became friends with Nura, a black woman from Liberia. Her real name was Letabrihyan. She called me Bolya. As with many of my prison friendships, this one also started from the window ledge. It was difficult for us to communicate as her Arabic wasn't very good and neither was mine, despite the course I had done.

Nura always watched the five o'clock news and made a point of keeping us informed if she saw anything related to our case. For instance, she told us that an entire delegation from Bulgaria was in Libya to help us. She was generous to a fault. When she had a handful of washing powder, for example, she always gave us half of it.

She had been arrested along with ten others for an attempted plane hijacking. One of them had died in prison and she hoped that someone would live to tell their story. She claimed they were innocent and I honestly believed her. The only incriminating evidence they had on her was that she had a can of pepper spray with her on the flight. "Bolya, Bolya, we are *sua-sua*! We are the same," she would say.

Fatma Redzhab was a nasty piece of work and she was in a cell near ours. She went out of her way to proclaim our guilt to anybody who would listen.

"Why did you do this to the children? Why did you inject the children?" she would ask loudly when a large number of prisoners were within earshot.

I immediately bristled: "I haven't done anything!"

"Well, that's not what I heard," she said.

"I don't care what you heard."

"If I have heard you are guilty, then you are guilty," she would retort.

Fatma constantly tried to humiliate me and every time she saw me she started with the refrain: "Here comes the AIDS nurse. Hide your babies everyone. The AIDS nurse is coming."

Then Mabruka was moved into her cell. She did not tolerate Fatma teasing or talking badly of me. "You listen to me," she said. "Valya is my friend. You will not tell her what she did or didn't do. The court will decide if she is guilty. We are all equal here."

Fatma was a real criminal. She had robbed a bank and managed to transfer thousands of dollars to accounts outside Libya. It grated me that this low-life could accuse me of being a criminal when I had done nothing wrong. Thus, the cell Mabruka and Fatma shared became a strange symbol of the contradictory attitudes exhibited toward us in the Zhdeyda prison.

While hanging out the window one day, I met Rabia. She had a little boy called Mohammed. He had been born prematurely and as such he was small for his age. She would bring him and hand him to us through the bars so that we could play with him. I loved playing with the children. They kept me sane. These little children's hugs and kisses soothed the soul and eased the horrors of prison life. Even though we could not get away from the filth, rats and screaming women, these children helped us to remember that we had family and friends that loved us in the world outside.

When Mohammed was one year old, Rabia sent him to an orphanage. At Easter the Greek Patriarch from The People's Court sent us a cake and some painted eggs, which were delivered by someone from the embassy. Rabia was allowed to visit Mohammed at the orphanage so we gave her a few of the painted eggs and the cake to give to him. At the home a Bulgarian woman cooed over Mohammed's present, saying to him, "Wow, where did you get these painted eggs from?"

"Well, I am friends with the Bulgarians in prison," Rabia cut in. "Some people from their embassy brought these things and they gave some to Mohammed."

"Oh, God," the woman cried. "My child is in an orphanage. I haven't seen my child for three years and nobody gives me anything. Yet, there are people who send eggs to those murderers."

Rabia relayed this conversation to us even though it pained her to do so. I cursed that woman. Apparently there were still Bulgarians who didn't believe we were innocent and had no compassion for our undeserved imprisonment. I went berserk.

"Let her come here and say this to my face!" I yelled.

Trying to calm me down, Rabia said: "Well, I told her that if she wanted eggs so badly, she should come to jail."

Mabruka also comforted me and I cried on her shoulder. She told me to forget that insensitive woman's comments. I was still feeling down later that day and after lunch I went to Mabruka's cell and flopped onto Fatma's bed. Fatma stood in the corner watching me as I poured my heart out. She didn't tell me to get off her bed or make any of her typical disparaging remarks. No doubt she didn't want to face another rebuke from Mabruka, my friend and confidante.

I thank God that we met. I will never ever forget Mabruka.

Freedom in Prison

On 4 February 2002 we were ordered to pack our luggage and were taken from Zhdeyda. We took everything we could, even cans of water, because we didn't know where we were going. We were driven to a police station in Benghazi, then led to a house that was in the prison yard. The first floor was used by the police as offices. The second floor was to be ours. Compared to our previous 'accommodation', these cells were luxurious. The rooms were carpeted and had two beds and a wardrobe in each. In one of the rooms there was a television. It was like a dormitory.

When we arrived at 'The House', Saleh Abdel Salam of GICDF greeted us. I thanked him profusely for organizing our transfer: "You brought us here—you're like the sun!" Afterwards Valentina berated me. "How could you say he is like the sun? He is blacker than the devil," she said. Nevertheless, we all agreed that our new lodgings were a vast improvement.

Zdravko was also brought to The House. He and Kristiyana shared a room, Valentina and I cohabited and Nasya and Snezhana shared the third. We argued vehemently that Ashraf should also stay with us and eventually he was also moved to The House. Although conditions here were better than at Zhdeyda, we could hear the savage *a blanco* beatings carried out on prisoners downstairs. During this time we saw Gaddafi's son on a television broadcast categorically denying that Libya still tortured suspected criminals.

We had a fully equipped kitchen and Zdravko was allowed a small piece of ground to start a vegetable garden. We were effectively under house arrest. Initially, we were brought food from a nearby restaurant but later the guards would bring us bags of groceries. We relished being able to cook tasty meals, especially after the blandness of prison rice and noodles. Kristiyana would usually make the evening meal but we all took turns making our specialities. Mine were pizzas, *mekitsas* (batter-coated snacks), pastries and buns. Valentina had a sweet tooth and made cakes and cookies. Nasya made potato salad, fried fish and macaroni. As a result we all gained weight and stopped looking emaciated.

Kristiyana's and my birthday are in March (hers on the 12th and mine on the 14th) and we had 'real' parties with cakes and snacks. At the same time, celebrating our birthdays at The House made us aware that we were not free and might not live to our next birthday.

Despite the privileges we were afforded at The House, time dragged by and we struggled to keep ourselves busy and stimulated.

Every few weeks we would travel to the Indictment Chamber for our trial. This time there was only one judge and one public prosecutor. We couldn't fathom why we were being treated so well. It was astonishing that we were flown to the trial by private jet, along with our new lawyer, Plamen Yalnazov, and the public prosecutor. Perhaps the Libyans thought that as such high-profile criminals we needed protection from potential assassination. Or perhaps they were manipulating the international community's perceptions, making an obvious demonstration of how well they were treating us.

While GICDF was sponsoring lavish flights, Gaddafi himself was making statements to the press such as: "I know Bulgaria and the work of Bulgarians. For decades they have worked well in Libya, with no incidents. I am bewildered how Bulgarians could do this."

It *was* utterly bewildering.

A year and four months of boredom ensued. We watched a lot of television in that time, often seeing our faces on the news. Wednesday was the highlight of our week as we were allowed visitors. Embassy representatives visited often. Once a year family members could visit.

I was ecstatic when Emil arrived to see me. Then my two daughters came. Gery stayed in Libya for two weeks and the police drove her to and from the prison.

Only one colleague from the children's hospital visited us—Katya, Nasya's roommate at the dormitory. Two or three of Valentina's friends would also visit regularly. I didn't know them from before and generally left them to catch up.

At one stage, I was hospitalized for an operation. I developed bladder cancer while in prison. The Bulgarian nursing staff were very sympathetic to our plight and after I was discharged, they regularly visited The House.

At Easter and Christmas the Greek Orthodox Church would send a priest to chat with us. They were the only ones who offered us spiritual support. I had never been particularly religious before my incarceration, although I had read many books on spirituality. I was philosophical about karma, about God. In prison I started fasting and thinking about God. Mabruka's strong faith had inspired me. I now believe that there is only one God, whether your call it Allah, Buddha, God, whatever.

I knew our fate was out of our hands and I prayed that God would help us.

Case No. 213/2002

The charges in our case, case no. 213/2002 were: deliberately infecting 393 Libyan children with HIV; causing an AIDS epidemic in the El-Fatih hospital in Benghazi; extramarital relations; production, distribution, use and possession of alcohol and conducting illegal currency exchanges. We had an opportunity to rebut these absurd charges during our first trial and testified that the confessions made by Nasya, Kristiyana and Ashraf were false and extorted through violence. Amazingly, the state set about prosecuting the people involved in our torture.

On 25 June the prosecution began presentation of its case. Thankfully, this time the proceedings were much more orderly than before and we were not verbally and physically assaulted by the parents of infected children. As far as I could tell, only two parents were admitted into the courtroom. We stayed in our 'cage' while Nasya took the stand. The prosecution tried to twist Nasya's words so as to discredit her. She simply told the truth and it served us well.

Each day when we arrived at court we were met by hordes of angry parents bearing placards such as: 'Nurse Kristiyana, what have we done to you that you infected our children with AIDS?', 'We thought that nurses were angels but they made us sick!' and 'Bandits have human rights but we only have Allah!'. I saw incredible pain and desperation in these people's eyes. And utter hatred. They needed answers. They needed someone to blame for this tragedy—and we were the obvious scapegoats.

The Indictment Chamber in Benghazi referred our case to the criminal court on 26 August. The charges were divided into four major groups: AIDS related; currency crimes; violation of moral codes and production and consumption of alcohol.

Another year passed. During the first hearing in 2003, Bulgarian journalists were admitted to the proceedings. While the trial dragged on, a series of political moves were being made by our Foreign Minister, Solomon Passy, who met with various representatives of the Libyan Government. Passy visited us whenever he could and would keep us informed of any developments. He even assisted Ashraf, who by now could speak Bulgarian fluently, with applying for his Bulgarian citizenship.

He told us how GICDF, together with the Bulgarian authorities, had managed to persuade Professor Luc Montagnier to appear as a witness for the defence. Our joy was overshadowed by reports that the number of infected children at the hospital had risen to 413. So many lives were ruined or lost while this courtroom charade played out.

The BTA (Bulgarian News Agency) correspondent wrote extensively on the participation of and support given by European experts:

'On 3 April, the Italian scientist and AIDS researcher Professor Vittorio Colizzi gave an interview to BBC World. The scientist was called to give an expert opinion in connection with the preparation of a 2002 report by Professor Luc Montagnier, the co-discoverer of HIV. The report was commissioned by the Libyan authorities and aims to establish the causes of the epidemic in the Benghazi hospital in the period 1997-98. "This infection has signs of a hospital infection. It occurred in the hospital due to a child who was treated for other diseases, but was a carrier of the AIDS virus. Then there was an exchange of blood material between that child and other children. All this happened in 1997 or even before that," Vittorio Colizzi said. The reason for the rapid spread of the infection was the fact that this type of virus proved to be particularly pathogenic, according to the research report. The source of this type of virus is considered to be the countries of the Sahara Desert. It is believed that it was brought to Libya by immigrants from Chad or Cameroon. "In 1997 the virus was already present in the Benghazi hospital where the Bulgarian nurses started work a year later and this is the only sure thing," the professor claimed. He claimed that during the epidemic the medical staff in Libya did not have information about AIDS or about the means to protect against the virus. The comment by Minister Solomon Passy on the following day read: "The information in the report by Professors Luc Montagnier and Vittorio Colizzi proves the innocence of the Bulgarian medics detained in Libya. I personally believe that this report will have an important and positive influence on the decisions that we expect the judiciary in Libya to take."'

The biggest names in the field of AIDS epidemics thought we were innocent—what a relief! The world would not allow a travesty of justice to occur and such concrete evidence would surely acquit us. We believed that even the most prejudiced judge would be swayed by Colizzi's and Montagnier's findings.

Easter came and went. We wanted to believe Passy's reassurance that this would most likely be our last Easter in prison, but then a Libyan woman suffering from AIDS gave damning testimony, claiming that Ashraf had infected her.

You remember Ashur ... one of my favourite children from the paediatric ward? His father was also discovered to be HIV-positive. However, he never blamed me for his illness. In fact, he tried to visit me in prison to see how I was holding up. He would tell anyone who would listen that we were the victims of a hospital cover-up. Walid, the boy with 'fish skin', didn't forget me either. He visited me several times at The House. He told me that he had been questioned and pressured to testify against me. He refused. His support meant so much to me.

On 6 July 2003 we were unexpectedly moved from The House to the Kuefiya prison in Benghazi. The prison adjoined the court. All our belongings were left behind. We were jailed in the city where more than

400 children from the El-Fatih Hospital had been infected with AIDS and their parents were convinced that this was our fault.

All seven of us were housed in a detached building which had previously been used by the prison management. It was almost exactly in the middle of the prison. We had two rooms, not cells, with just one bed in each. During the day the doors were unlocked and we could hang out in the 'garden' in front of the building. Initially we had to stay in the prison itself due to an unscrupulous guard who was 'letting' our rooms to inmates. Once, in the presence of several other officers, I told him off. "Hey! What do you think this is ... a market? How much did that one from yesterday give you to bring her here?" I asked. "This cell is reserved for us Bulgarians. Is she Bulgarian?"

He was furious. He complained about my behaviour to his superiors and then to the consulate. A diplomat came to see him, his superior and me to find out what was going on. Before the guard could make any kind of accusation, I interjected: "This guard rents out our cell to the other inmates. How much money did she give you to accommodate her?" I said, turning to the policeman.

He stopped letting our cell. He made it obvious that he hated me. I didn't care. I knew that he couldn't torture me now. There were too many people supporting us and checking up on how we were being treated. I laughed when I heard the other policemen talking about the incident. "You know what Valya said to him? If you only saw how she said it to him," they scoffed. I am not a cruel person by nature but mocking him was my way of exacting revenge for all that I had suffered. I could not reconcile myself to fitting into the guard-prisoner hierarchy.

A week after settling in to Kuefiya, the claim for damages filed by a group of parents of HIV-infected children was concluded. They were awarded 10.7 million dollars by the state. In coming years many parents would file similar claims.

Luc Montagnier and Vittorio Colizzi finally appeared as witnesses for the defence on 3 September. Their examination took two days. On the second day Vittorio Colizzi said: "I am ninety-nine percent convinced of the innocence of the Bulgarians. The expansion of the AIDS epidemic in Libya after 1997 is probably also due to negligence in the El-Fatih hospital in Benghazi."

On 7 September we exercised our right to have a 'last word' before the judge. We were brief: "We are hopeful and look forward to seeing how the testimony of the scientists will be accepted!" Two weeks later, our lawyer and the prosecution presented their closing arguments. BTA provided a detailed analysis of the arguments presented by the defence and prosecution. The prosecution's arguments are summarized here:

- The prosecution based its indictment on the confessions of the defendants, Ashraf al-Hadjudj, Nasya Nenova and Kristiyana Vulcheva, given during the preliminary investigation in 1999. The defendants claimed that they were part of an organization with the help of which 500 to 1,000 children in Libya were contaminated with HIV.

- The second piece of evidence referenced by the prosecution was the exhibit of five banks of plasma protein which, according to the previous trial's testimony, were found at Kristiyana's home. According to a study protocol conducted on two of the banks, they may have contained the HIV virus in a pure form and in high concentrations.

- The testimony and reports of Libyan doctors and Abu Dadzhadzha Aud, coordinator of the National AIDS Committee in Libya, were used by the prosecution. These reports highlighted that the spread of the infection in 'such an exemplary facility is unnatural and there are many scientific arguments which indicate foul play occurred at the children's hospital, El-Fatih, in Benghazi'.

In the indictment the prosecutors made seven claims:

- The number of infected children grew rapidly in a relatively short period of time and the probability of infection being transmitted through re-use of an infected needle is low—between three and 1,000 cases per annum;

- The presence of 4 subtypes of the virus is unnatural. In an epidemic there are usually no more than one or two subtypes. Furthermore, the region in which the outbreak occurred, the Socialist People's Libyan Arab Great Jamahiriya, does not have a large HIV-positive population.

- The absence of HIV among the mothers of the HIV-positive children highlighted the unnatural cause of the infection and supported the idea that the children were infected through injections of high doses of HIV.

- Rapid HIV tests were conducted and positive HIV results emerged minutes after testing the children's blood, rather than the usual half an hour later, and indicated that the virus was in unnaturally high percentages.

- The infection was concentrated in certain sectors of the hospital, with no plausible explanation for why this was the case.

- The infection occurred in the paediatric hospital. Unlike with adults, children do not question why they need injections and cannot generally recognize malicious intent. The laboratory studies conducted by the World Health Organization found that many of those infected were not carriers of the hepatitis B virus— implying that the infection was not caused by contamination and sterility issues as infection with the hepatitis virus is much more easily transferred than HIV. The prosecution argued that the infection of the children should therefore be assumed to have been caused by deliberate acts.

Plamen Yalnazov's arguments for the defence, as captured by BTA, follow:

- Nasya's confession is an essential component relied upon by the prosecution. All of the Bulgarians' confessions do not contain any probative value. On 9 February 1999 a large group of Bulgarian citizens were arrested by Libyan authorities and, according to the detention protocol, which was presented as evidence, the decision to detain and take the group to the Head Investigation Directorate/MID was only made on 12 April of the same year.

- In another protocol it is recorded that on 11 March 1999 the detainees were interrogated using dogs at the MID in Tripoli. According to the testimony of two officers from the investigative group, the detainees were physically and psychologically tortured during interrogations. Court transcripts from the trial at the Indictment Chamber in Benghazi reveal that forensic medical experts testified that the detainees were subjected to torture.

- The defendants were questioned at the General Investigation and Prosecution Bureau for National Action and on 14 April 2000 they were housed at the Zhdeyda prison in Tripoli until they then were relocated to the Police Dogs School in the Libyan capital. When they were initially questioned, no witnesses were present nor physically identified them. The defendants were not entitled to protection or to make complaints about their unlawful detention.

- According to Article 304 of the Criminal Procedure Code of Libya, 'failure to comply with the requirements of law relating to the exercise of essential procedural steps will lead to the annulment of the evidence collected on the base of these actions'. The practice of the Supreme Court of Libya mandates: 'a reference to the confession should be done selectively and should not be taken into account when obtained by illegal means and intimidation, however convincing it may seem'.

- Concerning the allegations related to finding five bags containing plasma protein at Kristiyana Vulcheva's house, the report by Dr al-Bashir Allagi shows that two of them were infused with HIV in its purest form and in large concentrations. According to the documentation regarding the search, it was carried out on 15 April 1999, yet the content of the banks was recorded on 2 and 15 February of the same year.

- None of the documentation presented by the prosecution provided reliable medical proof that the discovered plasma protein material did in fact contain the AIDS virus.

- The report by Abu Dadzhadzha Aud stated that in a hospital such as El-Fatih, in-hospital infection is not possible. However, the World Health Organization (WHO), which visited the hospital in 1998, concluded that there were no infection control measures in place, sterilization was not efficient, there was a lack of supplies and the medical personnel's knowledge about the spread of AIDS was insufficient.

- The prosecution indicated that only between three and 1,000 people are infected with AIDS per annum through being injected with an infected needle. This was not accurate. This particular statistic was firstly applicable to European cities and secondly, referred to the number of HIV-positive people that receive injections. Moreover, WHO states that the use of injection as a method of treatment is the main cause of in-hospital infections in many countries. It estimates that 96,000 people are annually infected with HIV via injections.

- Regarding the allegation that the patients exhibited 4 subtypes of HIV, the lawyer argued that studies conducted on the patients actually showed that they were infected with HIV-1.

- The prosecution stated that the small number of infected mothers of sick children proved that the virus was artificially introduced. However, the defence stated that 40% of the mothers have not been subjected to AIDS tests. The rapid HIV test conducted on the children detects antibodies to the HIV virus and no information was provided to substantiate in what proportion these antibodies appeared. Further, rapid HIV tests cannot determine when or how a person was infected.

- In response to the prosecution's argument that the disease spread in only two wards of the hospital, namely where the Bulgarian nurses worked, Plamen Yalnazov demonstrated that the infection was detected in all but two wards of the hospital. There is no data on whether hospitalized children or children entering the hospital already had the disease.

- The fact that the infection occurred in a paediatric institution and not in a general hospital was explained by the fact that El-Fatih was the only facility of its kind servicing children from Cyrenaica and the region from Sirte to Tobruk.

- The prosecution's accusation against the 'Bulgarian team' does not clarify why other Bulgarian nurses were not involved the case. Moreover, in over 100 interviews with the infected children's parents, they indicate that the children were admitted and treated by nurses from the Philippines, Hungary, Poland and Libya.

- Based on this, as well as on the lack of evidence to support the allegations, the defence argued that the defendants could not be held responsible for causing the epidemic through malicious intent or medical error and subsequently asked for an acquittal on all charges and for the judge to dismiss the civil claims.

Autumn passed, winter came. We spent our fifth New Year's Eve in jail. Then spring, then Easter again ...

On 15 April we found out that the delivery of the verdict was to be postponed to 6 May, the day of Saint George the Victorious. It is a national holiday in Bulgaria and celebrates the valour of the Bulgarian Army. We believed that the Libyans deliberately made important announcements on our public holidays—Christmas, New Year's Day, Easter and so on—to further undermine us.

Deep down we knew that the outcome of this trial was in the hands of Muammar al-Gaddafi, regardless of the facts proving our innocence. At court, the judge seemed nervous. He was visibly trembling. He started to deliver the verdicts in Arabic.

With no interpreter at hand, we could just make out our names. Then Ashraf shouted: "No! It's a death sentence for all of us!" We couldn't believe it. My heart plummeted and I slumped against the bars of the cage. I dimly heard voices yelling *"Allahu Akbah*! Allah is great!" Then I saw a woman faint. The journalists swarmed toward the cage.

"How are you?" one asked.

"How do you feel?" asked another.

"Do you accept the verdict?" a man questioned, scribbling on his notepad.

Snezhana replied, "At the moment I can't tell the nightmare from reality."

"We are in hell," Nasya added.

We were evacuated quickly.

"Fast! Go, go, go. Quickly," a policewoman shouted, pushing us from the cage.

We were escorted back to the prison and shoved into an office. Phones began to ring incessantly, no doubt from journalists trying to get interviews. We were instructed to call our relatives. It was mayhem.

Emil and my children wept bitterly and I tried to calm them down, saying that this sentence was to appease the Libyan public and we had hope that it would be set aside. A kindly policeman had said to us earlier in the day that, "Whatever you hear today, know that it is for the people only."

I clung to these words, praying that they were true.

Zdravko didn't receive a death penalty and was released. He was found innocent of infecting the children with HIV and only the illegal currency crimes were upheld. He was given four years in prison, but, as he had already served this time, he was free to go. Journalists rushed to interview him when he left the court. On television later that day we saw Zdravko say: "I feel bad. I am not happy. I cannot say that I feel a bit happy because I am as innocent as the rest. Everybody is innocent! I promise that I will fight to the end and I ask for your help. I will fight for the liberation of those girls who remain here. For five years they have been in prison. The Libyans are making a mockery of justice, them, our country and of the whole world. After five years of hellish torment, beatings, all this pressure and all these unlawful atrocities, they send me away, wishing me all the best. And so I fight for them. I will fight!"

We were to be shot for being mass murderers.

Dead Women Walking

The whole world opposed the sentences and the United States and the European Union reacted sharply, criticizing Libya's judicial processes. The Libyan Prime Minister, Shukri Ghanem, commented to an Italian newspaper, *Corriere della Sera*, that, "The idea of a fair trial comes from the West, it does not come from Libya. It is believed that there should be a court, prosecution and defence. The law has been applied strictly in this trial. With regard to humanity, it is better to talk first and foremost about the children: there are more than 400 infected children. More than forty have already died and more continue to die. There are people guilty of that."

When my daughter Gery visited me, I asked her how our family and friends at home were doing.

"If I tell you something, promise you won't get angry," she pleaded. I agreed, not knowing what to expect. "Grandfather died two years ago," she said.

I was stunned. My father was dead.

"What are you telling me? What happened?"

"Someone found him three days after he died," she said, choking back the tears. "He didn't live to see you free."

My heart was breaking but I bottled my emotions inside. We only had half an hour for the visit. After she left I sobbed. I would never see my father again.

On 25 January 2005 the appeal trial commenced with the trials for the 'lesser' crimes running concurrently. What happened in the courtroom was a blur. I was emotionally numb. In the same month, I received more bad news: Ashur had died. He was seven. His whole family was infected: his mother was dying and his sister had tested positive for HIV.

Several days later, the parents of twins Shafaa and Marua Gaddafi filed a suit against the state and its medical institutions. The claim was for five million Libyan dinars. The reaction from other affected parents was like an avalanche and soon there was a class action—they demanded payment of huge sums of money, insisting that we were liable and that the state must therefore repeal our death penalties.

In the spring Gaddafi addressed a conference in Algeria, saying: "About the Bulgarians who killed our children ... I swear that Western officials have come to demand their release, saying: 'We want to take them with us now!' We told them that on the day that the court sentenced the nurses to death in Benghazi, there were demonstrations in support of the verdict. Then the West told us, 'He doesn't care about the opinion of our nation.' It is as if our nations are sheep and Libya gets to have no public opinion."

We realized we were doomed ...

Meanwhile, thirteen doctors from Benghazi reported that they had evidence that the perpetrators of the AIDS infection in the children's hospital were people from the security services and the Libyan health authorities. However, they were only willing to testify if the proceedings were moved outside of Libya and they were included in a witness protection programme. Of course, nothing like that happened.

We had no real hope that our death sentence would be repealed and waiting for death turned out to be a terribly boring occupation. The only things we were allowed to do were to eat and sleep.

Our meeting with President Georgi Parvanov was highly publicized. I doubt that many people realized that this meeting was largely politically motivated—and unpleasant. Before seeing us, he visited the infected children and then attended all sorts of meetings. We waited for him for eight or nine hours in an office at the police station. When we were introduced he was distant but cordial. He advised us that we should tell our story to the press. We asked whether he could organize us a telephone, which he did. That was pretty much it.

He didn't show sympathy or interest in us. He left us with a bitter taste in our mouths. He certainly didn't inspire confidence that things would get better.

Our occasional meetings with Solomon Passy, on the other hand, were welcome. He went the extra mile, arranging to meet outdoors in a tent and ensuring that we got to talk to our relatives and receive visits. He took a sincere interest in our welfare. He had met with Gaddafi three times and we really felt that he was doing everything in his power to get us released. We always felt much better after meeting with him and were so grateful for his efforts.

The US diplomat John Negroponte wanted to meet with Gaddafi to discuss our case and to visit us. Libyan authorities would only allow him to do so if he visited the sick children first. He refused to be dictated to and so his requests were denied.

Finally 31 May arrived—the day we would hear whether our death sentences would be repealed. The courtroom was crowded with representatives from various countries. It lasted only minutes. The judge deferred making his decision for another six months. Leaving the court, we were met by angry cries of: "There is no other God but Allah", "Bulgarians are enemies of Allah", "Kill them with bullets", "Death for Kristiyana" and "Bizzanti is a dog!"

A week later the criminal court of Ain Zahra in Tripoli found the nine Libyan policemen and 'The Chemist' not guilty of torturing us. The monsters that had dragged us through hell were free to go and we remained locked up. It was absurd.

We were moved back to Zhdeyda, where we shared a cell with my friend Mabruka and another inmate Seta. Ashraf was housed in the men's section. Mabruka told us that when we were transferred from

Zhdeyda a year and four months before, rumour had it that we would be released so that huge financial compensation could be paid to the suing parents. Then they heard that we wouldn't be released because the authorities in Tripoli were afraid of creating too many millionaires in Benghazi, where there was strong political opposition.

We spent three months cohabiting with Mabruka and Seta while a new wing was built especially for us. It comprised two large cells. Initially, our group stayed in one with a few Libyans in the other. Then another floor was added and after three months we had both cells to ourselves. It had a small yard in front of it as well as a hall where we could meet privately with diplomats. There was also a kitchen and a room we converted into a living room, using the modest armchairs and TV donated by our embassy.

Overall, the conditions were good, albeit tarnished by the fact that we had a bird's eye view of the executions they conducted twice a year about 100 metres away from our wing. The day before we would hear who would be killed, what time and how. In the morning we listened to shouts, shots and the moaning of grieving relatives.

On Christmas Day of 2005 we arrived at the court in Benghazi to hear whether the death penalty would be lifted or upheld. The death sentences were repealed! However, our joy was short-lived as a week later, on 1 January 2006, Gaddafi pointed out that the death penalty was by no means off the table for us in our appeal trial: "If the court confirms the death sentences of the Bulgarian nurses, they will be executed!" he said.

Our appeal trial started soon after. I was horrified that Ahmed's mother, Jamelia, testified against us. Especially as she had visited me in prison and told me that I "was his favourite". She swore on the Koran that she had seen Nasya, Ashraf, Snezhana and I injecting children a few beds away from Ahmed's. These children were already HIV

-positive when she allegedly saw us infecting them but the court did not acknowledge this. I was simultaneously angry and hurt. No amount of blood money could justify her actions. When she died of an AIDS-related illness on the first day of Ramadan, I couldn't help but think that Allah was exacting his vengeance for using his name in vain.

A month later we heard that a research team from the University of Oxford had been analyzing the blood samples from the infected children for three years and had established irrefutable evidence of our innocence. I was not excited at the 'break-through'. We would be let down again, I reasoned.

ళా ళా ళా

19 December 2006. The court acquitted us of all charges ... with the exception of deliberately infecting 400 children with HIV. We were sentenced to death—again. I had been in prison for almost seven years. Every last shred of hope disappeared; we would die branded child murderers. All those years in court had achieved nothing. It would have been better to have just killed us at the outset. It would have spared us and our families much emotional turmoil.

Again the world protested Libya's ruling. The support was important to us, but it accomplished nothing. We were going to die.

On Christmas Day in Bulgaria, in the capital of Sofia, all the lights were extinguished to show the country's support and compassion. Vidin, Veliko Tarnovo and Dobrich followed suit.

On the first day of the New Year, our country finally joined the European Union. The first words welcoming Bulgaria into the European community were about us ... the Union held the firm opinion that we were now its citizens and must be released.

Nicolas Sarkozy, then running for the French presidency, gave the following speech on 14 January 2007: "I want to be president of a France that advocates human rights. Every time a woman is tortured anywhere in the world, France must stand by her side! If they elect me for president, France will stand behind the Bulgarian nurses."

Several days later, the European Parliament adopted a resolution of support for us. There were a resounding 567 votes 'for' the resolution, one 'against' and seven abstentions. Even the Muslim organization, World Leadership of the Islamic Nation, pleaded for Muammar al-Gaddafi to prevent our execution.

Gaddafi, however, had no intention of pardoning or releasing us without getting something in return. On 4 February, eight years after we had been kidnapped, a Libyan website published the following information, quoted by BTA: 'There are secret negotiations underway to exchange the medics in Libya for the Lockerbie bomber. The negotiations involve Libya, Britain, Italy and other EU countries. Bulgaria is not mentioned.' According to the media coverage, our lives were being bartered for the return of a terrorist plus billions of dollars in compensation for the families of the infected children.

A month later another charge was instituted against us—this time for defamation. We couldn't believe it. Djuma Misheri and Abdul Madjit Schol, the two men responsible for our torture and humiliation, were suing us!

Fortunately, three and a half months later the court acquitted us of these charges, thereby acknowledging that we had been tortured.

On 10 July 2007 we anxiously paced up and down our cell, killing time, with the exception of Snezhana, who had broken her knee and was in plaster. The following day we would learn how we were to be executed. I went to the prison hospital with Snezhana. Her cast was supposed to be removed but the presiding GP was absent.

"She must come back in three days," a nurse instructed.

"But tomorrow is our verdict," Snezhana protested. "Give me a note saying that I can't go, please!"

"Why can't you go?" she sneered. "It's only court."

We phoned the embassy for advice and were told that she should not go to court with a broken leg.

In the evening one of the jailers, Idris, came to our cell. Making conversation, I asked him what he thought our sentence would be. With a crooked smile and a malicious glint in his eyes, he said, "Freedom." He was taking the mickey out of us. I responded calmly, "May God kill you quickly."

The next morning the director of the prison came to our cells and saw that Snezhana was still in bed.

"Get up!" he ordered. "Today is your sentencing."

"I'm not getting up. I'm not going anywhere," she insisted.

"You're going, or else ..."

They argued and I could see the director was furious. She realized she didn't have a choice and started to get dressed. The director stood in the doorway watching her. We tried to distract him so that she could have some privacy.

"What is your name?" Valentina asked.

"Do you have family?" I queried. "What sentence will they give us today?

"Death," he replied, drawing his hand across his throat in a gesture of being beheaded. "But they won't kill you. Soon you'll be going home," he added.

On the way to the court, we learned that GICDF had announced that the families of the HIV-infected children had received financial compensation. "We came to a reasonable compromise with the families," the GICDF director Saleh Abdel Salam said. "This agreement satisfies all parties and puts an end to this crisis."

Again no interpretation was provided when the judge passed our third sentence. We heard our names then a word we were already familiar with: *Byulada*. Death. They still didn't say how we would be executed—whether we would be hanged, shot or given a lethal injection.

In prison we waited to die. We put aside our petty quarrels and made an effort to peacefully live out our last days. We knew that any day could be our last. Whenever any of us were called out of the cell, we would mentally prepare ourselves for the end—only to discover that the captain wanted us to change a bandage, help a prisoner or take someone's temperature. Sometimes we were called away to assist with translating Bulgarian. We were so frightened. To live in suspense like that was indescribable. Someone being taken away to sew a button would cause palpitations, terror and a flurry of prayers. These incidents were even scarier than being taken to be interrogated knowing full well what pain lay ahead.

One day a few Turks were executed—shot. One of them had lived in a cell with Ashraf. He gave Ashraf his belongings to send to the Turkish Consul, who would pass them on to his family. He had spent ten years in prison and maintained that he was innocent. For more than a year after the executions Ashraf was constantly agitated. It was like they had shot one of us.

It sharply brought home our own reality and impending execution.

We are not Alone

We had endured eight years of indifference and negligence from our politicians and thousands of false promises. The five of us felt abandoned and betrayed by our country. However, on New Year's Eve of 2006, a few days after our second death sentence was pronounced, we learned of the 'You Are Not Alone' campaign. We saw on television thousands of Bulgarians supporting us, wearing ribbons and stickers displaying the Bulgarian colours. People from all backgrounds and ages shouted "You are not alone!" into the camera.

The campaign grew rapidly in Bulgaria as Bulgarian TV stations began broadcasting videos of support. They were shown worldwide. In some of them there were photo montages of us. Under our names (excluding Zdravko's), the captions read 'Sentenced to death'. We watched our tormented faces on TV and listened to our own voices as if they were telling somebody else's story.

Kristiyana: Just know that we are innocent and the only thing we want is freedom ...

Me: After each electric shock I thought I was dying. I never thought I would survive.

Snezhana: All the horror is written on my face.

Valentina: It has been too long ... too long.

Nasya: I want to go home.

Zdravko: It's enough!

On 9 February 2007 an organized concert was held in support of us, titled 'You Are Not Alone'. I can't describe how we felt watching this concert. This was one of the most important and moving moments in our lives. Seeing thousands of people supporting us and listening to the song written for us and performed by dozens of Bulgarian stars, we finally believed it—we were not alone! Our compatriots believed in us.

The concert was staged in front of Alexander Nevski, the biggest church in Bulgaria. Huge posters were displayed: 'Bulgaria will never abandon you', 'We are all with you!' and 'We wait for you to come home!' they read. Tens of thousands of voices shouted "Freedom, freedom, freedom!" The commentator said that not a single performer who was invited refused.

The song 'You Are Not Alone' made every single one of us cry. People knew and believed that we were innocent. Seeing this show of solidarity, I was euphoric and proud to be Bulgarian. At that moment happiness infused every fibre of our bodies and souls. I wanted to shout it from the rooftop. I ran to call the policewomen: "Come here! Come here and see. We are not alone! This is for us. Everyone knows that we are not guilty."

I was shouting, yelling and embracing everyone. I translated to our jailers what was happening. One of the other Bulgarians, I can't remember who, joked with me, "Come on, shut up for a while. Because of you we can't hear anything. Why did you drag the cops here?"

Even the Arab TV stations began broadcasting the concert and reported the massive support we were getting. Libyan prisoners and jailers came upstairs shouting: "Sisters, see, this is all for you—you're not alone!"

Frankly, I didn't believe that we would be released. I knew that we would die in Libya. Despite that, I was really happy that so many people knew we would die innocent of the charges.

Mabruka was moved to a prison in her home town because she had only three years left of her sentence and was already on a lighter regime. I regularly talked on the phone with her. We were entitled to twenty-minute calls to Bulgaria on Sunday and Wednesday; on Monday and

Thursday we could make local calls, usually to the embassy. This time I used my twenty minutes to talk to Mabruka.

"Valya, all of us here watched you on TV!" she told me. "We gather together and pray for you and I tell them: 'Here she is, Valya, my friend.' Everyone believes in you. You will go home soon—the whole world is behind you."

"Yeah, right, we're not going home with three death sentences. They will definitely kill us and probably soon because of all the attention we're getting."

"No, they won't! You're going home," she reassured me.

Let us go home? No chance, I thought.

The campaign swiftly gained momentum. In America, we were often featured on CNN and many celebrities publicly supported us. Soon, buildings all over Europe were sporting 'You Are Not Alone' ribbons and posters.

We were touched that the nursing staff at two hospitals in Brussels observed two minutes of silence to express their support for us. We watched broadcasts of organized protests in England, France and Belgium and it wasn't just Bulgarians that took part in them: the Western world was behind us too. George Michael even cancelled a concert in Germany because of us and instead sang to tens of thousands of Bulgarians. He spoke 'to us' for a few minutes, saying "You are not alone!" Then he sang 'Freedom' … what we were dreaming about and longing for most.

Benita Ferrero-Waldner, the Commissioner for External Relations and European Neighbourhood Policy in the EU, visited us often. We were restricted by what we could say in front of the Libyans so we developed an excellent body-language dialogue. What we said out loud was one thing and what we said with our eyes was another. She asked me about the tapestry I was working on, but really was asking whether everything was okay. She kept telling us, "Just a little bit longer, just a little bit longer."

In Bulgaria, the campaign reached fever pitch. Television presenters wore ribbons on their clothes while reading the news. Politicians also wore ribbons. We watched a news report on how the fire engines in Sofia would sound their sirens as a gesture of support. We watched whole classes of children telling us, "You are not alone!"

Friends, family, colleagues and strangers sent us hundreds, possibly thousands, of letters, *martenitzi* (a traditional Bulgarian yarn decoration) and other things that showed their support. They sent little reminders of the world outside—like vials of beach sand, pebbles and shells. We literally had boxes full of correspondence. Sometimes they were addressed to individuals and sometimes to the group. It didn't matter. We read everything. We set Ashraf's letters aside and gave them to the officers to pass on to him.

Piles of letters would arrive each day. When we were finished reading the embassy would collect our mail—there was no room to store it in the cell. And every day new letters would come in their place. We kept our favourites. I treasured a letter from a young child. I read and reread it and it moved me to tears. It said:

'Aunt Valya! I am eight years old and can imagine what it is like for you. Since I was born, you have been in jail. I know that one day you will come out of there and I hope this will be before my next birthday.'

I hope so too, I thought. I hope so too!

The Embrace

On 11 June 2007 we had quite an unexpected visit from Cecilia Sarkozy, wife of the newly elected President of France. We liked her immediately and could tell that she was very smart.

"Thank you very much for your husband prioritizing us in his presidential campaign," I said.

"I am not here so you can thank me," she interrupted. "I've come to take you away from here!"

We had heard tens, maybe hundreds of similar promises. I do not know why but I instinctively bought into her words. After this meeting, I couldn't stop talking about her. Sighing melodramatically, Nasya said, "Valya, everybody promises, everybody lies—you get your hopes up for nothing."

The First Lady of France told us that she would return in twelve days and she kept her promise.

A few days before this meeting we had been presented with a document stating that neither we nor our families would sue the Libyan Government for compensation. The British Ambassador, the EU Ambassador and Mitko Dimitrova from our embassy were in attendance and urged us to sign it. Valentina, Ashraf and I refused. The others were furious with us. This was obviously the road to freedom. We didn't feel that our freedom should be dependent on this condition. Then Mitko told us: "Listen, until all of you sign, nobody gets out of here!"

We were not allowed to tell anybody about the document and were sent away with it to sign in our own time. When Cecilia Sarkozy first visited us, we wanted to tell her about the document and ask for advice but didn't because we had been sworn to secrecy. However, it became apparent that she knew all about the declaration and that we had not signed it. Very gravely she instructed us: "Sign it right away. I need this document. Without it, I can't help you. The Libyans want to get rid of you as soon as possible."

Valentina and I realized we had no choice but to sign. We conceded that we would dance to Libya's tune till the end, whatever that would be. I cannot sue them, but after the years of emotional turmoil in Libyan courtrooms, I don't want to.

On 23 July 2007, we learned that Benita Ferrero-Waldner and Cecilia Sarkozy were in Tripoli. Throughout the day I was restless. Her words reverberated in my mind: "I've come to take you away from here; I've come to take you away from here!" played over and over. Snezhana and I were sitting in the cell and kept talking about that.

"Valya, today is the day. I can feel it," Snezhana said. "She's coming for us."

"Yes, Snezhana. Of course, she's going to take us away," I answered, although I didn't think this was likely. I so much wanted it to be true but my rational mind told me that we wouldn't ever leave prison, at least not alive.

To distract myself, I started sewing a tapestry of Saint George.

"Valya, come watch the news. They're talking about whether we will leave or not," one of the girls called to me.

"No," I replied. "Not until I'm done sewing the eagle of Saint George. I'm staying put. It will help us," I added.

"Well, come sew it here. There are turbulent negotiations underway with this schizophrenic Gaddafi!"

"I'm staying put until I finish what I have started!" I responded.

Finally, at around 6pm, I made the last stitch and the image of Saint George was finished. The sewing had kept me calm and had put me into a kind of trance. The tapestry was very good. I began kissing it, my talisman.

"We're going home!" I declared. "Saint George will help us." I called the others to see it but it didn't lift their spirits as it had done mine.

"Valya, we're not going anywhere. The negotiations are not going well. They say Benita and Cecilia will stay another night in Tripoli."

That evening we all went to bed early, bitterly disappointed that the negotiations for our release had apparently failed. I fell asleep thinking that all my hopes were stupid. At best I would spend the rest of my life in a Libyan jail; at worst, I would be executed or thrown to a kangaroo court comprising the parents of the infected children.

At about half past four in the morning, the light in our cell was turned on. Kristiyana's hand was on my shoulder. She told me not to be scared. "The *mudir* told us we have three hours to get ready to leave."

"Where to?" I asked.

"I don't know."

In the dimness I heard Valentina mutter, "Oh God, where will they drag us now?"

"We're going home," I shouted.

"Yes, we're going home," Kristiyana said softly. Her words had a hollow ring to them.

We longed for freedom so badly. We told ourselves that we were being released, when the reality was that it was unlikely.

The *mudir* arrived at the cell. He said that we had to have our fingerprints taken and to sign some documents. Kristiyana yelled, "I'm not going anywhere without someone from the embassy being here." She was promptly handed a phone, which she used to dial Mitko Dimitrova, the Bulgarian diplomat who had worked tirelessly on our case. We adored him. "What? Really?" she squealed into the mouthpiece. Turning to us she told us that Zdravko was in Sarkozy's private plane. A miracle!

I wanted to go to the bathroom to get dressed. Valentina beat me to it.

She was notorious for spending ages in the bathroom. We would often joke that she slept in there. Suddenly Mitko arrived. He had obviously been talking to Kristiyana on a mobile phone on the way. "Valentina, come out of the bathroom," he shouted. "You're all leaving! You don't want to be left behind, do you? You, Valya. Come as you are."

"But I'm in my pyjamas," I objected.

"It doesn't matter. We'll find you something to put on."

We were taken to the police admin office. The policemen were bustling around. They grabbed my hands and took my prints. They pushed a piece of paper in front of me. Mitko said "Sign!" and I obeyed. It turned out that it was my release form. I couldn't think clearly—I merely followed orders.

I went back to the cell, which had turned into a madhouse. It was crammed with journalists, photographers, cameramen and several police. Valentina was still in the bathroom.

"What is that noise?" Valentina shouted. "Get these people out of here. I can't come out of the bathroom!"

"Come out, Valentina. They'll leave us here because of you. Dressed or not, we have to go, Slowgine."

The cell was getting more and more crowded. At some point Ashraf appeared as well. "Valya, what is happening?" he pleaded. "Nobody has told me anything."

"Ashraf, help take these bags out, please," I requested. "By the time this slowgine finally comes out of the bathroom it will be daylight." He was still waiting for me to answer his question.

"We're going home," I said, embracing him.

We then went to the prison common room, where we waited for an hour and fifteen minutes before our transport arrived. Unlike other nights, the lights were off and there was no one around. I remembered what Mabruka had said to me seven years earlier: "Gaddafi's son will pay off the parents to keep them quiet and one night you will fly out of here and no one will see you." I very much wanted to shout, "Mabruka, you were right!"

We walked with our luggage toward the exit. I mentally noted that this would be the last time our feet touched this prison floor; the last time our bodies would be behind bars; the last time we breathed the prison air; the last time we smelled the fear and filth of the prison. I didn't get to say goodbye to any of the prisoners, jailers or policemen who had gradually come to believe in our innocence and to respect us. Their many faces drifted through my mind like a photo montage—I said imaginary goodbyes to each one of them and embraced them. I became tearful thinking about them. I had one person that I desperately wanted to bid farewell to, but couldn't: Mabruka. She had been my closest friend through all these nightmarish years. She never forgot me, never refused to help me, never failed to say that we were innocent ... I vowed that one day I would see her again and give her the hug that I couldn't then.

Our group squashed into three jeeps. I was between Valentina and Nasya. I squeezed Valentina's hand. I couldn't help but remember that the last trip where we had been so tightly packed: when we were kidnapped from the children's hospital in Benghazi eight and a half years ago. We were all incredibly nervous.

When we left the women's section of the prison, we saw the French ambassador's car waiting for us. My heart was filled with relief and joy. I could feel it pounding with excitement. We would be free soon!

Driving to the airport, we didn't see a soul on the streets. It was like we were travelling through a ghost town. When we arrived at the airport, we saw a French plane parked on the runway. Cecilia Sarkozy, Benita Ferrero-Waldner and Marc Pierini were standing on the stepladder a few dozen metres away. Freedom was within our grasp—we couldn't quite believe it. As we were getting out of the jeeps, a man shouted in Arabic, "No touching your luggage!" My heart stopped.

We were roughly pushed into some kind of hall by Libyan policemen. Ambassadors from almost all the European Union countries were present. One of the suited men came up to us and asked, "Ashraf, what do you want to do? Do you want to stay in Libya or do you want to go to Bulgaria?"

"I want to go to Bulgaria," he said. "Please. I'm a Bulgarian from now on."

The man began working on some documents. Seeing this, a Libyan policeman said, "Come on, you're ready. Go home."

We left everything in Libya—luggage, clothing and sadly our letters and the Saint George tapestry. We ran toward the aeroplane, waving goodbye to the British Ambassador. We stopped quickly to squeeze Mitko's hand on the runway. Then we saw, just centimetres from the plane's stepladder, a living barrier of Libyan police. I thought that perhaps the Libyans were tricking us and would shoot us for attempting to escape.

However, I then noticed that Abdul Salam from GICDF was also there. I shook his hand and thanked him for helping us. He smiled and instructed the soldiers to step aside.

On the plane there were dozens of people. There was an entire French delegation, plus Benita, Cecilia and Marc Pierini. We received a warm welcome and we were quickly told to take our seats as they wanted to leave as soon as possible. Cecilia Sarkozy was talking on the phone with her husband and said to him twice, "I have got them with me, all seven of them."

Kristiyana was sitting close to her and she handed her the phone. "Tell my husband that you are all here, please," Cecilia instructed.

"Yes, all seven of us are on the plane," Kristiyana beamed.

We noticed that our French companions looked haggard and were on edge. The celebratory mood quickly evaporated.

At precisely 6:25am on 24 July 2007, the plane took off from Libyan soil. We were on our way to Bulgaria!

It turned out that the negotiations of the past forty-eight hours had been anything but smooth sailing. Gaddafi insisted that the European Union commit to making a sizeable contribution to the Benghazi International Fund and in exchange we would be extradited to serve out our sentences in Bulgaria. He kept demanding more and more. In addition, a private agreement was reached with the affected families regarding compensation. At around 12pm the previous night, Gaddafi had asked for an exorbitant sum. Cecelia had snapped at her aids, "I can't take it! He is constantly changing his mind. I'm going to the plane; if need be, without the Bulgarians! What more does he want?"

Benita was in charge of negotiating the prisoner-exchange agreement between Bulgaria and Libya. Benita had a copy of the Arabic text and the Libyans had a copy in French. Neither document had any value if the respective translation was not signed. At 3pm they had brought Zdravko to the airport. He had been holed up at the British Embassy. Then the work began to get us released. Marc Pierini had come to the jail in person three times and had been sent away because the police were still busy taking our fingerprints and so on. The whole release process was intense, fast and confused and there was an underlying feeling that Gaddafi might make further demands and put a stop to our extradition at any moment.

About an hour after our taking off the pilot announced that we had left Libyan airspace. Everybody breathed a sigh of relief. Then the champagne was cracked open. "Here's to freedom!" we cheered.

Ashraf was a Muslim and had never drunk alcohol before.

"Valya, what am I to do now?" he asked, looking at the people knocking back the contents of their flutes. I whooped with joy and, my voice trembling with emotion, said, "Drink up. Ashraf, we are free. Free!"

"Here's to freedom!" he exclaimed and took his first-ever sip of champagne. He grimaced but then drank the whole glass.

"Whisky, please," Valentina asked the air steward.

I saw Snezhana, Nasya, Kristiyana, Valentina, Zdravko and Ashraf through new eyes. We were no longer prisoners sentenced to death, just people. It was strange to see their smiles and to hear them laughing. I couldn't quite comprehend that we were free. My mind whirled with thoughts of what the future held and whether this nightmare was truly over.

The flight from Libya to Bulgaria is just over two hours' long. I was fascinated by the digital map displayed on one of the panels and avidly watched how the little image of our plane inched closer to Bulgaria. Suddenly the pilot announced that we were starting our descent. We were euphoric. The road from Libya to our country turned out to be so short, yet it had taken us eight and a half years to travel it ... The immeasurable suffering—physical, mental and spiritual—was over.

In Bulgaria it was already morning. The dark night of my first interrogation and my first torture—23 February 1999—was followed by 3,073 sunrises over eight and a half years that I barely noticed and certainly didn't appreciate. Now, I saw the sun rising over Bulgaria as though for the first time and marvelled at the miracle.

੭ৡ ੭ৡ ੭ৡ

Finally the plane landed. Looking out the window, I saw a huge crowd gathered on the tarmac. I got a lump in my throat when I heard Zdravko talking on the phone to his son Marian. "Yes, we are all here," he said.

"Who is with you? We will see each other now."

The plane finally stopped moving and the door was opened. The stepladder was lowered. The moment we had all been waiting for, longing for and dreaming about had finally arrived. We wanted to run into the crowd, to kiss the earth and to hug our loved ones.

We were impatient to get off the plane. According to protocol, the French delegation disembarked first. Then it was our turn. We passed dozens of politicians, ambassadors and diplomats from all the European countries while cameras flashed incessantly and journalists called our names.

Our new Foreign Minister, Ivaylo Kalfin, welcomed us. We barely registered the cameramen's booms overhead as we shook hands with various officials. We were walking on Bulgarian soil and were in absolute shock. Only a minute had passed but it felt like forever. I hurried toward the crowd and Marian barrelled into me and threw his arms around me.

After so many years imprisoned with his parents, I felt as though I knew him inside out. This tight embrace made me tremble with emotion. Cameras clicked around us, capturing photographs that became iconic. Marian let me go and I found myself face to face with my daughters. We cried with joy. I hugged them and never wanted to let go—first Gery, then Tony, then both so that the three of us merged into one. I was overwhelmed by my love for them. The thought of embracing my darling daughters had kept me alive and gave me the strength to withstand the torture and hopelessness of our situation.

At last we were free!

My New Life

The euphoria at the airport was huge. Relatives, strangers and reporters hugged us. Later we found out that television stations around the world had broadcast these extraordinary moments live. We heard that the Bulgarian President, Georgi Parvanov, had pardoned us—our slates were wiped clean and we were free as birds.

From the airport we were taken to the President's residence in Boyana. They allocated us different rooms. I was on the second floor.

"Mom, come for a walk in the garden," my kids urged.

"But ... will they let us? Who should we ask?" I spontaneously replied.

My daughters threw peculiar glances at me. I immediately realized what was wrong: I didn't have to ask permission for such a mundane thing as going for a walk. I had been conditioned to act like a child, I reflected bitterly. Only twenty-four hours before I couldn't do anything without permission—I went to sleep when I was told, my mealtimes were predetermined and I could only walk in the yard at set times. It was all very strange.

"Mom, you are free," they said gently. "You can go wherever you want. Let's walk." So we did. I constantly looked over my shoulder though, half expecting to be reprimanded.

The next day we were escorted to the Military Medical Academy. There was a police car in front of our van and an ambulance behind it. The sirens were on which scared my children. In Libya we had often been escorted by police and people had angrily thumped our car, so this was mild in comparison. "We're just going to the hospital," I soothed.

At the hospital a male nurse took me from one consulting room to another. He was wearing a military-issue camouflage uniform. It reminded me of being in Libya, except that this time it was a nurse not a policewoman who dragged me from place to place. We spent two or three days being examined by various doctors.

"How do you feel?" one asked.

"As in Libya," I replied truthfully. "You look like the policemen there."

I realize that this comparison was unfair.

The next day the doctor came dressed in a suit. I told him I liked his shirt. "I put it on especially for you. I don't want to remind you of Libya," he said.

The following day I went out with my daughter Gery and her boyfriend Tihomir to buy some clothes. I literally had nothing to wear. We went to a second-hand clothes market as we didn't have money for anything fancier. My list of what I needed included the most basic things like toothpaste, a toothbrush and underwear. An everyday thing like choosing a bra was difficult. I didn't know my bra size anymore. In prison I wore whatever I was given and clothes were worn to cover nakedness, not for comfort. Unashamedly, I lifted my blouse and told the sales assistant, "I need a bra to fit a bust like this."

She looked at me in shock. Gery and Tihomir shook their heads in disbelief. I realized then that I had forgotten what 'normal' behaviour was outside of prison. I couldn't undo what I had done. It was tragic; my body had escaped Libya, but my psyche was still dancing to its horrible tune. Today I don't like thinking about those initial few months back in Bulgaria. I'm sharing them only to explain how I felt.

The five of us continued to live together in Boyana for several months and left at around Christmas. We would make day-trips into Sofia, the capital. It seemed to have changed dramatically in our absence. There were a lot more people, shops, new buildings and shiny cars. When I visited my home town of Byala Slatina in northeast Bulgaria, however, it seemed as though time had stood still. The paediatric ward where I had worked before hadn't even replaced the trays the nurses used to carry syringes in the past ten years! (The window frames had been replaced although it was arguable whether it was an improvement.)

The first time I went to Byala Slatina was just a few days after we arrived from Libya. It rained and I couldn't get enough of the greenness of the town. The natural surroundings instantly made me feel relaxed. In Libya I had seen more than enough sand and desert. The familiar faces of neighbours, friends and colleagues welcomed me home. Everybody was delighted to see me. Even people that I didn't know very well came up to me in the street to tell me how happy they were that I had come back safely. Many former patients wished me well.

I never went alone to Byala Slatina. The thought of being on my own in a town made me panicky. One of my daughters always came with me. It took me a long time to get used to being around people and being in open spaces.

On our fortieth day in Bulgaria, a Saturday, my daughter Tony, Nasya and I went to a monastery near Bankya, about ten kilometres west of Sophia. The interior of the crumbling monastery was lit by soft candlelight and it smelled of incense. On entering, it was as though a weight was lifted from my heart. We lit several candles for the living and the dead and sat silently. I thought of my dad and prayed that he could see me now. I finally felt at peace.

I moved back into our home in Byala Slatina. It gradually became easier to interact with people. All my friends and neighbours started calling me and coming to my house. Life seemed to resume exactly where it had left off ten years before. However, the times had changed and I had not.

When journalist Martin Karbovski came to interview me, he caught me boiling compote over a small fire in the yard.

"Valya, don't you know that only poor people boil their own compote nowadays?" he teased.

"Well, Martine, I am poor. I haven't been working for ten years."

It seemed as though no one made their own winter supplies and compotes anymore. Why would they when they could just buy what they needed from the store? My practices may be outdated—it doesn't bother me—but fortunately my daughters still love my compotes and my pepper relish. I did try the store-bought equivalents but they taste artificial to me. Besides, my kids always want me to cook my specialties for them. I must be a very good cook or else they missed my cooking for so long and are making up for lost time.

I started working in the paediatric ward of the hospital again. Now I am not simply recognized by my name badge; the patients and staff all know me. Sevda had also returned to work at the hospital. She avoids me. We haven't talked about what happened in Libya but I don't care. I don't want to rake up the past.

When I first left for Libya it was with the intention of making money, but I had returned to my original poverty. In the first few months of being back, politicians bombarded us with promises, many of them regarding compensation. I am angry that the state has not fulfilled its promises to us. Nearly ten years ago when we were kidnapped and arrested, our government had been slow to react and when they did it seemed as though they were merely going through the diplomatic motions but really couldn't have cared less about us. They kept our plight secret and suggested we might be guilty. If they had reacted promptly I believe that we would have been spared the pain and indignity of being tortured and would not have lost so many years of our lives.

Our government spent a fortune to secure our release. Why didn't they do anything when we were first unjustly arrested? I feel that the government owes us because its initial inertia ultimately caused our suffering—and they seem to have recognized this fact. On the first day back from Libyan soil we met with the Health Minister, Radoslav Gaydarski, and Emiliya Maslarova, the Minister of Labour and Social Policy. There were cameras, embraces and promises. The politicians assured us that we would be financially compensated as we had obviously lost all form of income while we had been incarcerated. We would also be assisted in finding nursing positions. The government then promised to back-pay insurance for that time and told us that we would receive the maximum state pension for the rest of our lives. None of these things have happened in the two years that we have been home ... and we want what we were promised.

I work on an extremely low salary and I have a family to support. I have read in the newspapers and have heard on the streets that many Bulgarians believe we do not deserve monetary compensation from the government because our release cost so much. Some old people even blame us for their low pensions and others point out that we have already received many benefits (no doubt referring to the apartments donated to each of us by a private company, which, incidentally we are unable to live in as they have not been finished). We did receive a one-off grant of BGN10,000 from the state—hardly back-payment for eight and a half years considering that the average monthly salary for June 2007 was BGN515. I suppose I am lucky: the municipality of Byala Slatina gave me an additional 1,000 euros.

Everything was spent on house repairs. We can't even afford to take a short holiday to the seaside. It irritates me when people make these unfounded claims that we are being greedy, but I am learning to ignore these negative people. I prefer to think about the people who want to embrace me and support me. Thank God there are a lot of them.

Quite often strangers stop me on the street to tell me that they have always believed in our innocence. Even when we travelled to France with Bulgarian diplomats, people would recognize us and say: "We know you from television. We've been thinking about you a lot and are so happy that you are free!"

At the hospital I get many letters written by absolute strangers. Their kind words move me and are helping to heal the emotional wounds.

ôô ôô ôô

Many of the cruel characters in our story got their just desserts.

Mama Salma was forced to retire several months before we were released and came to say goodbye. She looked haggard. Ironically, she asked us for a glass of water because her former colleagues (and prisoners) wouldn't give her one. We obliged because we didn't want to be spiteful like she had been to us. We found out that one of her sons had hanged himself and the other had gone insane.

Ahmed's mother, Jamelia, had committed perjury. She died of AIDS. (Ahmed, sweet boy, was treated in Italy along with three hundred other infected children from El-Fatih Hospital. I don't know what happened to him after that and I hope he is still alive and well.)

Four hundred and sixty children were infected with HIV at the hospital. The families that lost children or whose children still live with the virus received one million dollars for their suffering—the EU maintains that it did not pay this compensation to the families. They suffered terribly and I feel sorry for them, even those who believe we got away with murder.

I hope those responsible for the epidemic at El-Fatih Hospital will be punished and that they have learned better medical practices, although I fear that this is not the case. A year after we were freed, five new cases emerged of children infected with HIV. The Libyans once again pointed fingers at us. Thankfully we were in Bulgaria—beyond their reach.

We never met Cecilia Sarkozy again but would like to. I have such immense respect for her.

I often think about Nura, who went home in early 2007 ... Mabruka will be free soon too. We regularly talk on the phone. Mabruka often tells me that she will find a way to visit me in Bulgaria when she is released. I eagerly await her visit and will welcome her with open arms.

I relish my freedom and enjoy my work as a nurse. My colleagues at the hospital have made me feel at home and are sensitive not to bring up the awful memories of Libya. I live frugally, but it doesn't matter. My greatest treasures are my loved ones. I am alive and free to walk the streets whenever I want and I never fail to thank God for this miracle.

I try not to dwell on what happened in Libya, but my nightmares mean I can never be wholly free from the memories. I have a recurring dream of being executed by a firing squad.

I'm an optimist though and hope one day to conquer the bad dreams.

Buns and Chocolate Cake

My first encounter with Valya Chervenyashka was more than strange. I was chief editor of the 'Psychic Challenge' TV show. In the original version of the show, one of the challenges required the participants to reveal the story of a stranger without even seeing them. I instantly suggested inviting one of the nurses who had recently been released from a Libyan jail. Their story had always moved me and right from the beginning of their ordeal I watched closely as events unfolded. The plot in which they were involved was absurd, outrageous, controversial and mostly unpredictable. There were many times during those eight-odd years that I thought they would be released and would describe what had REALLY happened to them.

I expected many books to be written on the topic of the 'Libyan case', especially by those involved. However, only Kristiyana and Snezhana have published their memoirs, which were very interesting but only recorded the facts. They didn't cover what I personally wanted to read—what it was like to be in their shoes. I suppose this was due to the speed with which the ghost writers compiled Kristiyana's and Snezhana's biographies.

We first contacted Kristiyana to see whether she would be willing to participate in the 'Psychic Challenge' TV show. She was busy that day we wanted to shoot so we approached Snezhana, who initially agreed but pulled out at the last moment. Valya was happy to be on the show. She thought it would be very interesting to see if the ten clairvoyants could tell what she had been through. Three of them were very accurate. She was surprised by the outcome as she hadn't expected such uncanny accuracy. She impressed me as being an objective, fair and tough person. I instantly liked her.

In between shoots we talked a lot. Naturally, we, the crew, were curious about her life in Libya and she answered our questions patiently, in detail and unemotionally, as if dispensing information on a random topic. I asked her why she hadn't published a book.

"No one has offered," she replied.

After we had wrapped up shooting I drove Valya back to Byala Slatina. By the time we stopped in front of her house I had already offered to write this book. She agreed. We met again a few months later when she was taking part in the 'You've Got Mail' show. We met a few days before the broadcast to select some excerpts from the letters written to her while in prison.

I got the sense that she was testing the water to see if I was the right person to tell her story.

After the 'Psychic Challenge' show ended a few months later, I took a break. I spoke with Valya at the beginning of July to arrange a meeting. She was fed up with journalists probing into her past and got annoyed when their questions revealed that they had not done their homework. I am not a journalist and I was not looking for sensational story angles. I *had* done my homework—I had read more than 1,000 pages on the case and had watched at least sixty hours of video footage. The chronology generated by the Bulgarian Telegraph Agency helped me a lot and when it was time to start working on the book, I felt ready for it.

Our first meeting took place in a bistro in Sofia. The conversation flowed smoothly and it didn't feel like an interview. To Valya's great indignation, I hadn't prepared a list of questions and simply let the conversation take its natural course. We jumped from one topic to another and from one point in time to another. I didn't want the book to necessarily follow the chronology.

Our next meetings were at Tony's house. I had already met her daughter when filming 'You've Got Mail'. Valya was more relaxed in this setting and revealed some of the horrific details of what had happened to her in prison.

When we started working together I left two things at home: my pity and my manners. I made her talk even when she was overcome by emotion. I kept asking for details about the smallest things so that I could visualize what she had been through.

Gradually the story began to shape. Valya never doubted what I did or the way I worked; she never complained when I asked her the same question for the tenth time. I think the fact that I had actually brought a list of questions to our second meeting finally won her trust.

Our meetings were very pleasant. She used to make me cup after cup of tea. Once she baked buns with cheese—the same type that she made in prison. Another time she treated me to a delicious chocolate cake. I snacked and she smoked. We didn't want her story to come across as melodramatic. We wanted to capture the various emotional aspects of her experiences and especially the unique relationships that resulted from her incarceration. Of course, a lot happened in those eight and a half years, but we didn't want to bombard the reader with too much information or to make the narrative heavy or boring. This book could offend or make many people angry in Bulgaria and abroad but Valya and I wanted to tell her story as she saw it.

During our second meeting I asked her why she agreed to tell me her story. She answered in her typically candid style: "Because you offered and when I promise to do something I do it."

The next day we met again. It was the day before the first anniversary of her return to Bulgaria and she reminded me of this.

I like Valya. She is an extremely strong, stable and honest person. She had been through hell and I have merely helped put her thoughts on paper. I hope that publishing this book will finally put a full stop to her long and painful saga.